There are some just sentiments, some repartees, a little pathos, and an excellent moral in this production;—but there are also vapid scenes, and improbable events, which, perhaps, more than counterbalance those which are lively and natural.

Had the punishment of the two fashionable women been inflicted by a less disgraceful means, than a prison for debt; and had the singular conduct of Lord and Lady Priory been supported by occurrences, as pleasantly singular, this might have ranked among some very deserving comedies: Yet even in its present imperfect state, assisted by the art of excellent acting, it was most favourably received on the stage; and may now, without the charm of scenic aid, afford an hour's amusement to the reader.

The character of Miss Dorrillon is by far the most prominent and interesting one in the piece; and appears to have been formed of the same matter and spirit as compose the body and mind of the heroine of the "Simple Story"—A woman of fashion with a heart—A lively comprehension, and no reflection:—an understanding, but no thought.—Virtues abounding from disposition, education, feeling:—Vices obtruding from habit and example.

This part was written purposely for Miss Farren; but the very season she should have performed it, she quitted the stage, to appear in a more elevated character.

DRAMATIS PERSONÆ

Lord Priory	Mr. Quick.
Sir William Dorrillon	Mr. Munden.
Sir George Evelyn	Mr. Pope.
Mr. Bronzely	Mr. Lewis.
Mr. Norberry	Mr. Waddy.
Oliver	Mr. Fawcett.
Nabson	Mr. Thompson.
Lady Priory	Miss Chapman.
Lady Mary Raffle	Mrs. Mattocks.
Miss Dorrillon	Miss Wallis.

Several Servants, &c.

SCENE:—London.

WIVES AS THEY WERE, AND MAIDS AS THEY ARE

ACT THE FIRST

SCENE I

An Apartment at Mr Norberry's.

Enter **SIR WILLIAM DORRILLON**, followed by **MR NORBERRY.**

MR NORBERRY
Why blame me?—Why blame me?—My sister had the sole management of your daughter by your own authority, from the age of six years, till within eight months of the present time, when, in consequence of my sister's death, she was transferred to my protection.

SIR WILLIAM
Your sister, Mr. Norberry, was a prudent good woman—she never could instruct her in all this vice.

MR NORBERRY
Depend upon it, my dear friend, that Miss Dorrillon, your daughter, came to my house just the same heedless woman of fashion you now see her.

SIR WILLIAM [Impatiently]
Very well—'Tis very well.—But, when I think on my disappointment—

MR NORBERRY
There is nothing which may not be repaired. Maria, with you for a guide—

SIR WILLIAM
Me! She turns me into ridicule—laughs at me! This morning, as she was enumerating some of her frivolous expenses, she observed me lift up my hands and sigh; on which she named fifty other extravagances she had no occasion to mention, merely to enjoy the pang, which every folly of her's sends to my heart.

MR NORBERRY
But do not charge this conduct of your daughter to the want of filial love:—did she know you were Sir William Dorrillon, did she know you were her father, every word you uttered, every look you glanced, would be received with gentleness and submission:—but your present rebukes from Mr. Mandred (as you are called), from a perfect stranger, as she supposes, she considers as an impertinence, which she has a right to resent.

SIR WILLIAM
I wish I had continued abroad. And yet, the hope of beholding her, and of bestowing upon her the riches I acquired, was my sole support through all the toils by which I gained them.

MR NORBERRY
And, considering her present course of life, your riches could not come more opportunely.

SIR WILLIAM
She shall never have a farthing of them. Do you think I have encountered the perils of almost every climate, to squander my hard-earned fortune upon the paltry vicious pleasures in which she delights? No; I have been now in your house exactly a month—I will stay but one day longer—and then, without telling her who I am, I will leave the kingdom and her for ever—Nor shall she know, that this insignificant merchant, whom she despises, was her father, till he is gone, never to be recalled.

Wives As They Were And Maids As They Are by Mrs Inchbald

A COMEDY, IN FIVE ACTS

AS PERFORMED AT THE THEATRE ROYAL, COVENT GARDEN

Elizabeth Simpson was born on 15th October 1753 at Stanningfield, near Bury St Edmunds, Suffolk.

Despite the fact that she suffered from a debilitating stammer she was determined to become an actress.

In April 1772, Elizabeth left, without permission, for London to pursue her chosen career. Although she was successful in obtaining parts her audiences, at first, found it difficult to admire her talents given her speech impediment. However, Elizabeth was diligent and hard-working on attempting to overcome this hurdle. She spent much time concentrating on pronunciation in order to eliminate the stammer. Her acting, although at times stilted, especially in monologues, gained praise for her approach for her well-developed characters.

That same year she married Joseph Inchbald and a few months later they appeared for the first time together on stage in 'King Lear'. The following month they toured Scotland with the West Digges's theatre company. This was to continue for several years.

Completely unexpectedly Joseph died in June 1779. It was now in the years after her husband's death that Elizabeth decided on a new literary path. With no attachments and acting taking up only some of her time she decided to write plays.

Her first play to be performed was 'A Mogul Tale or, The Descent of the Balloon', in 1784, in which she also played the leading female role of Selina. The play was premiered at the Haymarket Theatre.

One of the things that separated Elizabeth from other contemporary playwrights was her ability to translate plays from German and French into English for an audience that was ever-hungry for new works.

Her success as a playwright enabled Elizabeth to support herself and have no need of a husband to support her. Between 1784 and 1805 she had 19 of her comedies, sentimental dramas, and farces (many of them translations from the French) performed at London theatres. She is usually credited as Mrs Inchbald.

Mrs Elizabeth Inchbald died on 1st August 1821 in Kensington, London.

Index of Contents

REMARKS

The writer of this drama seems to have had a tolerable good notion of that which a play ought to be; but has here failed in the execution of a proper design.

Here are both fable and characters to constitute a good comedy; but incidents, the very essence of a dramatic work, are at times wanting, at other times ineffectual.

The first act promises a genuine comedy; and the authoress appears to have yielded up her own hopes with reluctance. In the dearth of true comic invention, she has had recourse at the end of her second act, to farce; though she certainly knew, that the natural, and the extravagant, always unite so ill, that in the combination, the one is sure to become insipid, or the other revolting.

Aware of this consequence, and wanting humour to proceed in the beaten track of burlesque, she then essays successively, the serious, the pathetic, and the refined comic; failing by turns in them all, though by turns producing chance effect; but without accomplishing evident intentions, or gratifying certain expectations indiscreetly raised.

The outline of a good play is a dangerous drawing to give to the public;—a feeble plan is the surest safe-guard for an indifferent work: want of talent is never so forcibly perceived, as when certain parts are imperfect, whilst the rest demand eulogium. Critics are nice, and sometimes enraged where they find at once, ability, and imbecile attempt to explain vigorous conceptions.

Happy the author whose imagination extends no farther than the produce of his own anxious efforts! Such an one knows not his danger—his incapacity; and escaping censure, enjoys with triumph implied success, or receives animadversion with a sense of injury: whilst the more judicious, though more humble writer, often shrinks from praise as unmerited, yet bears with still heavier heart the critic's reproach as his due.

MR NORBERRY

You are offended with some justice; but, as I have often told you, your excessive delicacy, respecting the conduct of the other sex, degenerates into rigour.

SIR WILLIAM

True; for what I see so near perfection as woman, I want to see perfect. We, Mr. Norberry, can never be perfect; but surely women, women, might easily be made angels!

MR NORBERRY

And if they were, we should soon be glad to make them into women again.

SIR WILLIAM [Inattentive to Mr. Norberry]

—She sets the example. She gives the fashion!—and now your whole house, and all your visitors, in imitation of her, treat me with levity, or with contempt.—But I'll go away to-morrow.

MR NORBERRY

Can you desert your child in the moment she most wants your protection? That exquisite beauty just now mature—

SIR WILLIAM

There's my difficulty!—There's my struggle!—If she were not so like her mother, I could leave her without a pang—cast her off, and think no more of her.—But that shape! that face! those speaking looks! Yet, how reversed!—Where is the diffidence, the humility—where is the simplicity of my beloved wife? Buried in her grave.

MR NORBERRY

And, in all this great town, you may never see even its apparition.

SIR WILLIAM

I rejoice, however, at the stratagem by which I have gained a knowledge of her heart; deprived of the means of searching it in her early years, had I come at present as her father, she might have deceived me with counterfeit manners, till time disclosed the imposition.—Now, at least, I am not imposed upon.

[Enter **SERVANT**.

SERVANT

Lord Priory.

[Exit.

SIR WILLIAM

Lord Priory!

MR NORBERRY

An old acquaintance of mine, though we seldom meet. He has some singularities; and yet, perhaps—

[Enter **LORD PRIORY**.

MR NORBERRY
My dear Lord, I am glad to see you. Mr. Mandred.
[Introducing **SIR WILLIAM**]
My lord, I hope I see you in perfect health.

LORD PRIORY
Yes; but in very ill humour. I came to London early this morning with my family for the winter, and found my house, after going through only a slight repair, so damp, that I dare not sleep in it: and so I am now sending and going all over the town to seek for lodgings.

MR NORBERRY
Then seek no further, but take up your lodgings here.

LORD PRIORY
To be plain with you, I called in hopes you would ask me; for I am so delicately scrupulous in respect to Lady Priory, that I could not bear the thought of taking her to an hotel.

MR NORBERRY
Then pray return home, and bring her hither immediately, with all your luggage.

LORD PRIORY
I am most extremely obliged to you [very fervently]; for into no one house belonging to any of my acquaintance would I take my wife, so soon as into yours. I have now been married eleven years, and during all that time I have made it a rule never to go on a visit, so as to domesticate, in the house of a married man.

SIR WILLIAM
May I inquire the reason of that?

LORD PRIORY
It is because I am married myself; and having always treated my wife according to the ancient mode of treating wives, I would rather she should never be an eye witness to modern household management.

SIR WILLIAM
The ancients, I believe, were very affectionate to their wives.

LORD PRIORY
And they had reason to be so; for their wives obeyed them. The ancients seldom gave them the liberty to do wrong: but modern wives do as they like.

MR NORBERRY
And don't you suffer Lady Priory to do as she likes?

LORD PRIORY
Yes, when it is what I like too. But never, never else.

SIR WILLIAM
Does not this draw upon you the character of an unkind husband?

LORD PRIORY

That I am proud of. Did you never observe, that seldom a breach of fidelity in a wife is exposed, where the unfortunate husband is not said to be "the best creature in the world! Poor man, so good natured!—Dotingly fond of his wife!—Indulged her in everything!—How cruel in her to serve him so!" Now, if I am served so, it shall not be for my good nature.

MR NORBERRY

But I hope you equally disapprove of every severity.

LORD PRIORY [Rapidly]

What do you mean by severity?

MR NORBERRY

You know you used to be rather violent in your temper.

LORD PRIORY

So I am still—apt to be hasty and passionate; but that is rather of advantage to me, as a husband—it causes me to be obeyed without hesitation—no liberty for contention, tears, or repining. I insure conjugal sunshine, by now and then introducing a storm; while some husbands never see any thing but a cloudy sky, and all for the want of a little domestic thunder to clear away the vapours.

SIR WILLIAM

I have long conceived indulgence to be the bane of female happiness.

LORD PRIORY

And so it is.—I know several women of fashion, who will visit six places of different amusement on the same night, have company at home besides, and yet, for want of something more, they'll be out of spirits: my wife never goes to a public place, has scarce ever company at home, and yet is always in spirits.

SIR WILLIAM

Never visits operas, or balls, or routs?

LORD PRIORY

How should she? She goes to bed every night exactly at ten.

MR NORBERRY

In the name of wonder, how have you been able to bring her to that?

LORD PRIORY

By making her rise every morning at five.

MR NORBERRY

And so she becomes tired before night.

LORD PRIORY

Tired to death. Or, if I see her eyes completely open at bed time, and she asks me to play one game more at piquet, the next morning I jog her elbow at half after four.

MR NORBERRY
But suppose she does not reply to the signal.

LORD PRIORY
Then I turn the key of the door when I leave the chamber; and there I find her when I come home in the evening.

SIR WILLIAM
And without her having seen a creature all day?

LORD PRIORY
That is in my favour: for not having seen a single soul, she is rejoiced even to see me.

MR NORBERRY
And will she speak to you after such usage?

LORD PRIORY
If you only considered how much a woman longs to speak after being kept a whole day silent, you would not ask that question.

MR NORBERRY
Well! this is the most surprising method!

LORD PRIORY
Not at all. In ancient days, when manners were simple and pure, did not wives wait at the table of their husbands? and did not angels witness the subordination? I have taught Lady Priory to practise the same humble docile obedience—to pay respect to her husband in every shape and every form—no careless inattention to me—no smiling politeness to others in preference to me—no putting me up in a corner—in all assemblies, she considers her husband as the first person.

SIR WILLIAM
I am impatient to see her.

LORD PRIORY
But don't expect a fine lady with high feathers, and the et cætera of an Eastern concubine; you will see a modest plain Englishwoman, with a cap on her head, a handkerchief on her neck, and a gown of our own manufacture.

SIR WILLIAM
My friend Norberry, what a contrast must there be between Lady Priory and the ladies in this house!

LORD PRIORY [Starting]
Have you ladies in this house?

MR NORBERRY

Don't be alarmed; they are both single, and can give Lady Priory no ideas concerning the marriage state.

LORD PRIORY

Are you sure of that? Some single women are more informed than their friends believe.

MR NORBERRY

For these ladies, notwithstanding a few, what you would call, excesses, I will answer.

LORD PRIORY

Well, then, I and my wife will be with you about nine in the evening; you know we go to bed at ten.

MR NORBERRY

But remember you bring your own servants to wait on you at five in the morning.

LORD PRIORY

I shall bring but one—my old servant, Oliver, who knows all my customs so well, that I never go any where without him.

MR NORBERRY

And is that old servant your valet still?

LORD PRIORY

No, he is now a kind of gentleman in waiting. I have had no employment for a valet since I married:—my wife, for want of dissipation, has not only time to attend upon herself, but upon me. Do you think I could suffer a clumsy man to tie on my neckcloth, or comb out my hair, when the soft, delicate and tender hands of my wife are at my command?

[Exit.

SIR WILLIAM

After this amiable description of a woman, how can I endure to see her, whom reason bids me detest; but whom nature still—

MR NORBERRY

Here she comes; and her companion in folly along with her.

SIR WILLIAM

There's another woman! that Lady Mary Raffle! How can you suffer such people in your house?

MR NORBERRY

She Is only on a visit for a few months—she comes every winter, as her family and mine have long been intimately connected.

SIR WILLIAM

Let us go—let us go. I cannot bear the sight of them.

[Going.

MR NORBERRY

Stay, and for once behave with politeness and good humour to your daughter—do—and I dare venture my life, she will neither insult nor treat you with disrespect. You know you always begin first.

SIR WILLIAM

Have not I a right to begin first?

MR NORBERRY

But that is a right of which she is ignorant.

SIR WILLIAM

And deserves to be so, and ever shall be so. I stay and treat her with politeness and good humour! No—rather let her kneel and implore my pardon.

MR NORBERRY

Suffer me to reveal who you are, and so she will.

SIR WILLIAM

If you expose me only by one insinuation to her knowledge, our friendship is at that moment at an end.

MR NORBERRY [Firmly]

I have already given you my promise on that subject; and you may rely upon it.

SIR WILLIAM

I thank you—I believe you—and I thank you.

[Exeunt **SIR WILLIAM** and **MR NORBERRY**.

[Enter **LADY MARY RAFFLE** and **MISS DORILLON**.

MISS DORILLON [Stealing on as **MR NORBERRY** and **SIR WILLIAM** leave the stage]

They are gone. Thank Heaven they are gone out of this room, for I expect a dozen visiters! and Mr. Norberry looks so gloomy upon me, he puts me out of spirits: while that Mr. Mandred's peevishness is not to be borne.

LADY MARY RAFFLE

Be satisfied; for you were tolerably severe upon him this morning in your turn.

MISS DORILLON

Why, I am vexed; and I don't like to be found fault with in my best humour, much less when I have so many things to tease me.

LADY MARY RAFFLE

What are they?

MISS DORILLON

I have now lost all my money, and all my jewels, at play; it is almost two years since I have received a single remittance from my father; and Mr. Norberry refuses to advance me a shilling more.—What I shall do to discharge a debt, which must be paid either to-day or to-morrow, Heaven only knows!—Dear Lady Mary, you could not lend me a small sum, could you?

LADY MARY RAFFLE

Who, I!

[With surprise]

—My dear creature, it was the very thing I was going to ask of you: for when you have money, I know no one so willing to disperse it among her friends.

MISS DORILLON

Am not I?—I protest I love to part with my money; for I know with what pleasure I receive it myself; and I like to see that joy sparkle in another's eye, which has so often brightened my own. But last night ruined me—I must have money somewhere.—As you cannot assist me, I must ask Mr. Norberry for his carriage, and immediately go in search of some friend that can lend me four, or five, or six, or seven hundred pounds. But the worst is, I have lost my credit—Is not that dreadful?

LADY MARY RAFFLE

Yes, yes; I know what it is.

[Shaking her Head.

MISS DORILLON

What will become of me?

LADY MARY RAFFLE

Why don't you marry, and throw all your misfortunes upon your husband?

MISS DORILLON

Why don't you marry? For you have as many to throw.

LADY MARY RAFFLE

But not so many lovers who would be willing to receive the load. I have no Sir George Evelyn with ten thousand pounds a year—no Mr. Bronzely.

MISS DORILLON

If you have not now, you once had: for I am sure Bronzely once paid his addresses to you.

LADY MARY RAFFLE

And you have the vanity to suppose you took him from me!

MISS DORILLON

Silence.—Reserve your anger to defend, and not to attack me. We should be allies by the common ties of poverty: and 'tis time to arm; for here's the enemy.

[Enter **SIR WILLIAM**, with **MR NORBERRY**.

SIR WILLIAM

They are here still.

[Aside to **MR NORBERRY**, and offering to go back.

MR NORBERRY [Preventing him]
No, no.

MISS DORILLON
I have been waiting here, Mr. Norberry, to ask a favour of you.

[He and **SIR WILLIAM** come forward.

Will you be so kind as to lend me your carriage for a couple of hours?

MR NORBERRY
Mr. Mandred—

[Pointing to **SIR WILLIAM**.

—has just asked me for it to take him into the city.

LADY MARY RAFFLE
Oh, Mr. Mandred will give it up to Miss Dorrillon, I am sure: he can defer his business till to-morrow.

SIR WILLIAM
No, madam, she may as well put off her's. I have money to receive, and I can't do it.

MISS DORILLON
I have money to pay, and I can't do it.

LADY MARY RAFFLE
If one is going to receive, and the other to pay money, I think the best way is for you to go together; and then, what deficiency there is on one side, the other may supply.

MISS DORILLON
Will you consent, Mr. Mandred?—Come, do, and I'll be friends with you.

SIR WILLIAM [Aside]
"She'll be friends with me!"

MISS DORILLON
Will you?

SIR WILLIAM
No.

MISS DORILLON
Well, I certainly can ask a favour of Mr. Mandred better than I can of any person in the world.

MR NORBERRY
Why so, Maria?

MISS DORILLON
Because, instead of pain, I can see it gives him pleasure to refuse me.

SIR WILLIAM
I never confer a favour, of the most trivial kind, where I have no esteem.

MISS DORILLON [Proudly]
Nor would I receive a favour, of the most trivial kind, from one—who has not liberality to esteem me.

MR NORBERRY
Come, Miss Dorrillon, do not grow serious: laugh as much as you please, but say nothing that—

SIR WILLIAM [To her, impatiently]
From whom, then, can you ever receive favours, except from the vain, the idle, and the depraved?—from those whose lives are passed in begging them of others?

MISS DORILLON
They are the persons who know best how to bestow them: for my part, had I not sometimes felt what it was to want a friend, I might never have had humanity to be the friend of another.

[Enter **SERVANT**.

SERVANT
Sir George Evelyn.

MR NORBERRY
And pray, my dear, whose friend have you ever been?

[Enter **SIR GEORGE EVELYN**.

Not Sir George Evelyn's, I am sure; and yet he, of all others, deserves your friendship most.

MISS DORILLON
But friendship will not content him: as soon as he thought he had gained that—

SIR GEORGE EVELYN
He aspired to the supreme happiness of your love.

MISS DORILLON
Now you talk of "supreme happiness," have you procured tickets for the fête on Thursday?

SIR GEORGE EVELYN
I have; provided you have obtained Mr. Norberry's leave to go.

MR NORBERRY

That I cannot grant.

MISS DORILLON
Nay, my dear sir, do not force me to go without it.

SIR WILLIAM [With Violence]
Would you dare?

MISS DORILLON [Looking with Surprise]
"Would I dare," Mr. Mandred!—and what have you to say if I do?

SIR WILLIAM [Recollecting himself]
I was only going to say, that if you did, and I were Mr. Norberry—

MISS DORILLON
And if you were Mr. Norberry, and treated me in the manner you now do,—depend upon it, I should not think your approbation or disapprobation, your pleasure or displeasure, of the slightest consequence.

SIR WILLIAM [Greatly agitated]
I dare say not—I dare say not. Good morning, Sir George—I dare say not.—Good morning, Mr. Norberry.

[Going.

MR NORBERRY
Stop a moment.—Maria, you have offended Mr. Mandred.

MISS DORILLON
He has offended me.

SIR WILLIAM [At the Door, going off]
I shan't offend you long.

MR NORBERRY [Going to him, and taking him by the Arm]
Stay, Mr. Mandred: Miss Dorillon, make an apology: Mr. Mandred is my friend, and you must not treat him with this levity.

LADY MARY RAFFLE
No, no apology.

MISS DORILLON
No, no apology. But I'll tell you what I'll do.

[Goes up to **SIR WILLIAM**.

If Mr. Mandred likes, I'll shake hands with him—and we'll be good friends for the future. But then, don't find fault with me—I can't bear it. You don't like to be found fault with yourself—You look as cross as any thing every time I say the least word against you. Come, shake hands; and don't let us see one another's failings for the future.

SIR WILLIAM
There is no future for the trial.

MISS DORILLON
How do you mean?

MR NORBERRY
Mr. Mandred sets off again for India to-morrow.

MISS DORILLON
Indeed! I thought he was come to live in England! I am sorry you are going.

SIR WILLIAM [With earnestness]
Why sorry?

MISS DORILLON
Because we have so frequently quarrelled. I am always unhappy when I am going to be separated from a person with whom I have disagreed; I often think I could part with less regret from a friend.

SIR GEORGE EVELYN
Not, I suppose, if the quarrel is forgiven?

MISS DORILLON
Ah! but Mr. Mandred does not forgive! no! in his looks I can always see resentment.—Sometimes, indeed, I have traced a spark of kindness, and have gently tried to blow it to a little flame of friendship; when, with one hasty puff, I have put it out.

SIR WILLIAM
You are right. It is—I believe—extinguished.

[Exit **SIR WILLIAM**—**MR NORBERRY** following.

SIR GEORGE EVELYN
A very singular man.

LADY MARY RAFFLE
Oh! if he was not rich, there would be no bearing him—Indeed, he seems to have lost all his friends; for, during the month he has been here, I never found he had any one acquaintance out of this house.

MISS DORILLON
And, what is very strange, he has taken an aversion to me.—But it is still more strange, that, although I know he has, yet in my heart I like him. He is morose to an insufferable degree; but then, when by chance he speaks kind, you cannot imagine how it sooths me.—He wants compassion and all the tender virtues; and yet, I frequently think, that if any serious misfortune were to befall me, he would be the first person to whom I should fly to complain.

LADY MARY RAFFLE

Then why don't you fly, and tell him of your misfortune last night?

SIR GEORGE EVELYN [Starting]
What misfortune?

MISS DORILLON [To **LADY MARY RAFFLE**]
Hush!

LADY MARY RAFFLE
A loss at play.—
[To **MISS DORRILLON**]
—I beg your pardon, but it was out before you said hush!

SIR GEORGE EVELYN
Ah, Maria! will you still risk your own and my happiness? For mine is so firmly fixed on you, it can only exist in yours.

LADY MARY RAFFLE
Then, when she is married to Mr. Bronzely, you will be happy, because she will be so?

SIR GEORGE EVELYN
Bronzely! has he dared?

MISS DORILLON
Have not you dared, sir?

LADY MARY RAFFLE
But I believe Mr. Bronzely is the most daring of the two.—
[Aside to **SIR GEORGE EVELYN**]
Take care of him.

[Exit.

SIR GEORGE EVELYN
Miss Dorrillon, I will not affront you by supposing that you mean seriously to receive the addresses of Mr. Bronzely; but I warn you against giving others, who know you less than I do, occasion to think so.

MISS DORILLON
I never wish to deceive any one—I do admit of Mr. Bronzely's addresses.

SIR GEORGE EVELYN
Why, he is the professed lover of your friend Lady Mary! or, granting he denies it, and that I even pass over the frivolity of the coxcomb, still he is unworthy of you.

MISS DORILLON
He says the same of you; and half a dozen more say exactly the same of each other. If you like, I'll discard every one of you as unworthy; but, if I retain you, I will retain the rest. Which do you chuse?

SIR GEORGE EVELYN

I submit to any thing, rather than the total loss of you—But remember, that your felicity—

MISS DORILLON [Sighing]

"Felicity! felicity!"—ah! that is a word not to be found in the vocabulary of my sensations!—

SIR GEORGE EVELYN

I believe you, and have always regarded you with a compassion that has augmented my love. In your infancy, deprived of the watchful eye and anxious tenderness of a mother; the manly caution and authority of a father; misled by the brilliant vapour of fashion; surrounded by enemies in the garb of friends—Ah! do you weep? blessed, blessed be the sign!—Suffer me to dry those tears I have caused, and to give you a knowledge of true felicity.

MISS DORILLON

[Recovering.] I am very angry with myself.—Don't, I beg, tell Mr. Norberry or Mr. Mandred you saw me cry—they'll suppose I have been more indiscreet—
[Stifling her Tears]
—than I really have. For in reality I have nothing—

SIR GEORGE EVELYN

Do not endeavour to conceal from me, what my tender concern for you has given me the means to become acquainted with. I know you are plunged in difficulties by your father neither sending nor coming, as you once expected: I know you are still deeper plunged by your fondness for play.

MISS DORILLON

Very well, sir! proceed.

SIR GEORGE EVELYN

Thus then—Suffer me to send my steward to you this morning; he shall regulate your accounts, and place them in a state that shall protect you from further embarrassment till your father sends to you; or shall protect you from his reproaches, should he arrive.

MISS DORILLON

Sir George, I have listened to your detail of the vices, which I acknowledge, with patience, with humility—but your suspicion of those which I have not, I treat with pride, with indignation.

SIR GEORGE EVELYN

How! suspicion!

MISS DORILLON

What part of my conduct, sir, has made you dare to suppose I would extricate myself from the difficulties that surround me, by the influence I hold over the weakness of a lover?

[Exeunt, separately.

ACT THE SECOND

Enter **TWO PORTERS** from an upper Entrance, bringing in Trunks; **LORD PRIORY** and **MR NORBERRY** following.

MR NORBERRY
Here, Stephens, why are you out of the way? Show the men with these boxes into the dressing-room appointed for my Lord Priory.

[A **SERVANT** enters on the opposite Side, and the **PORTERS** follow him off at a lower Entrance on that Side.

[Enter **SIR WILLIAM DORRILLON**.

SIR WILLIAM
My lord, I hope I see you well this evening.

LORD PRIORY
Yes, sir—and you find I have literally accepted Mr. Norberry's invitation, and am come to him with all my luggage.

[Enter **OLIVER**, with a small Box in each Hand.

LORD PRIORY
Follow those men with the trunks, Oliver.

MR NORBERRY
Ah, Mr. Oliver, how do you do?

OLIVER
Pretty well—tolerably well—I thank you, sir.

[Exit.

[Enter **SERVANT**.

SERVANT
Lady Priory.

[Enter **LADY PRIORY**.

LORD PRIORY [To her]
Mr. Norberry, our worthy host; and Mr. Mandred.

[She courtesies.

MR NORBERRY
I hope your ladyship will find my house so little inconvenient to you, as to induce you to make no very short visit.

LADY PRIORY
I have no doubt, sir, but I shall find, from your friendship, every comfort in this house, which it is possible for me to enjoy out of my own.

[Enter **LADY MARY RAFFLE** and **MISS DORRILLON**.

MR NORBERRY [Introducing them]
Lady Priory—Lady Mary Raffle—Miss Dorrillon—Lord Priory.

LADY MARY RAFFLE
Permit me, Lady Priory, to take you to the next room: we are going to have tea immediately.

LADY PRIORY
I have drank tea, madam.

MISS DORRILLON
Already! it is only nine o'clock.

LADY PRIORY
Then it is near my hour of going to bed.

[**LORD PRIORY**, **SIR WILLIAM**, and **MR NORBERRY**, retire to the Back of the Stage, and talk apart.

LADY MARY RAFFLE
Go to bed already! in the name of wonder, what time did you rise this morning?

LADY PRIORY
Why, I do think it was almost six o'clock.

LADY MARY RAFFLE [In amaze]
And were you up at six this morning?

LADY PRIORY
Yes.

MISS DORRILLON
At six in the month of January!

LADY MARY RAFFLE
It is not light till eight: and what good, now, could you possibly be doing for two hours by candle-light?

LADY PRIORY
Pray, Lady Mary, at what time did you go to bed?

LADY MARY RAFFLE
About three this morning.

LADY PRIORY
And what good, could you, possibly be doing for eleven hours by candle-light?

LADY MARY RAFFLE
Good! it's as much as can be expected from a woman of fashion, that she does no harm.

LADY PRIORY
But I should fear you would do a great deal of harm to your health, your spirits, and the tranquillity of your mind.

[**MR NORBERRY** goes off—**LORD PRIORY** and **SIR WILLIAM** come forward.

LADY MARY RAFFLE
Oh, my Lord Priory, I really find all the accounts I have heard of your education for a wife to be actually true!—and I can't help laughing to think, if you and I had chanced to have married together, what a different creature you most likely would have made of me, to what I am at present!

LORD PRIORY
Yes; and what a different creature you most likely would have made of me, to what I am at present.

SIR WILLIAM
Lady Priory, I am not accustomed to pay compliments, or to speak my approbation, even when praise is a just tribute; but your virtues compel me to an eulogium.—That wise submission to a husband who loves you, that cheerful smile so expressive of content, and that plain dress, which indicates the elegance, as well as the simplicity, of your mind, are all symbols of a heart so unlike to those which the present fashion of the day misleads—

MISS DORILLON
Why look so steadfastly on me, Mr. Mandred? Do you pretend to see my heart?

SIR WILLIAM
Have you any?

MISS DORILLON
Yes; and one large enough to hold—even my enemy.

[Enter **SERVANT**.

SERVANT
Mr. Bronzely.

MISS DORILLON
Show him into the other room.

[Exit **SERVANT**.

Come, Lady Priory, we must introduce you to Mr. Bronzely: he is one of the most fashionable, agreeable, pleasant, whimsical, unthinking, and spirited creatures in all the world: you'll be charmed—

LADY PRIORY

I dare say it's near ten o'clock. I am afraid I shan't be able to keep awake.

MISS DORILLON

You must—We are going to have a little concert—'Twill be impossible to sleep.

[Exit **MISS DORRILLON**, leading off **LADY PRIORY**.

LADY MARY RAFFLE

Upon my word, my lord, your plan of management has made your wife unfit for company.

LORD PRIORY

So much more fit to be a wife.

LADY MARY RAFFLE

She is absolutely fatigued with hard labour—for shame!—How does household drudgery become her hand?

LORD PRIORY

Much better than cards and dice do yours.

[Exit **LADY MARY RAFFLE**, followed by **LORD PRIORY**—**SIR WILLIAM** is left on the Stage alone.

SIR WILLIAM

She "has a heart large enough to receive her enemy."—And by that enemy she means her father.

[He sits down, and shows Marks of Inquietude.

[Enter **SIR GEORGE EVELYN**.

SIR GEORGE EVELYN

I beg your pardon, Mr. Mandred—I hope I don't interrupt you—I only wished to speak to Miss Dorrillon.

SIR WILLIAM

She is just gone into the next room.

SIR GEORGE EVELYN

To the concert?

SIR WILLIAM

Are not you invited?

SIR GEORGE EVELYN

Yes; but before I go in, I wish to know who are the company.—Can you tell whether—a Mr. Bronzely is there?

SIR WILLIAM
I know he is.

SIR GEORGE EVELYN
Are you acquainted with him?

SIR WILLIAM
I have met him here frequently.

SIR GEORGE EVELYN
And are you certain he is here at present?

SIR WILLIAM
I have reason to be certain.

SIR GEORGE EVELYN
Any particular reason?

SIR WILLIAM
Your mistress, when his name was announced, went out, exclaiming, "he was the most charming and accomplished man in the world."

SIR GEORGE EVELYN [Greatly agitated]
She loves him, sir—I have reason to believe—to know she loves him. Thus she gives up my happiness and her own, to gratify the vanity of a man, who has no real regard for her; but whose predominant passion is to enjoy the villanous name of a general seducer.

SIR WILLIAM [Rising]
Why do you suffer it?

SIR GEORGE EVELYN
Hush! Don't repeat what I have said, or I lose her for ever. I am at present suffering under her resentment; and have just sent into the next room, to ask, if she were there, to speak with her.

[Enter **MISS DORRILLON**.

MISS DORILLON
And is it possible I was sent for by you?

SIR GEORGE EVELYN
Don't be offended, that I should be uneasy, and come to atone—

MISS DORILLON
I can't forgive you, sir; 'tis impossible.

[Going.

SIR GEORGE EVELYN
You pardon those, Maria, who offend you more.

SIR WILLIAM
But an ungrateful mind always prefers the unworthy.

MISS DORILLON
Ah! Mr. Mandred, are you there?
[Playfully]
And have you undertaken to be Sir George's counsel? If you have, I believe he must lose his cause.—To fit you for the tender task of advocate in the suit of love, have you ever been admitted an honourable member of that court? Have you, with all that solemn wisdom of which you are master, studied Ovid, as our great lawyers study Blackstone? If you have—show cause—why plaintiff has a right to defendant's heart.

SIR WILLIAM
A man of fortune, of family, and of character, ought at least to be treated with respect, and with honour.

MISS DORILLON
You mean to say, "That if A is beloved by B, why should not A be constrained to return B's love?" Counsellor for defendant—"Because, moreover, and besides B, who has a claim on defendant's heart, there are also C, D, E, F, and G; all of whom put in their separate claims—and what, in this case, can poor A do? She is willing to part and divide her love, share and share alike; but B will have all or none: so poor A, must remain, A, by herself, A."

SIR GEORGE EVELYN
Do you think I would accept a share of your heart?

MISS DORILLON
Do you think I could afford to give it you all? "Besides," says defendant's counsellor, "I will prove that plaintiff B has no heart to give defendant in return—he has, indeed, a pulsation on the left side; but, as it never beat with any thing but suspicion and jealousy; in the laws of love, it is not termed, admitted, or considered—a heart."

[Going.

SIR GEORGE EVELYN
Where are you going?

MISS DORILLON
To the music-room, to be sure: and if you follow me, it shall be to see me treat every person there better than yourself—and Mr. Bronzely, whom you hate, to see me treat him best of all.

[Exit.

SIR GEORGE EVELYN

I must follow you, though to death.

[Exit.

SIR WILLIAM
Fool! And yet am not I nearly as weak as he is? Else why do I linger in this house? Why feed my hopes with some propitious moment to waken her to repentance? Why still anxiously wish to ward off some dreaded fate?—If she would marry Sir George, now—if she would give me only one proof of discretion, I think I would endeavour to own her for my child.

[Enter **MR BRONZELY**, in haste.

MR BRONZELY
My dear sir, will you do me the greatest favour in the world?—you must do it in an instant too. Do, my dear sir, ask no questions; but lend me your coat for a single moment, and take mine—only for a moment—I cannot explain my reasons now, my impatience is so great;—but, the instant you have complied, I will inform you of the whole secret; and you will forever rejoice that you granted my request.

[Pulling off his Coat.

SIR WILLIAM [Aside, with great Scorn]
And this very contemptible fellow is the favoured lover of my daughter!—I'll—
[After a Struggle]
—yes—I'll make myself master of his secret—it may possibly concern her—my child—my child's safety may depend upon it.

MR BRONZELY
Dear Mr. Mandred, no time is to be lost!

SIR WILLIAM
This is rather a strange request, Mr. Bronzely. However, your fervency convinces me you must have some very forcible reason.—There's my coat, sir.

[Gives it him.

MR BRONZELY
Thank you, dear sir, a thousand times.—This goodness I shall for ever remember—this binds me to you for ever!

[Putting it on.

Thank you, sir, a thousand times!

[Bowing, dressed, and composed.

SIR WILLIAM [After putting on the other Coat]

And now, sir, explain the cause of this metamorphosis?—let me have the satisfaction to know what advantage will accrue from it; and in what I have to rejoice?

MR BRONZELY
Will you promise me not to reveal the secret, if I trust you with it?

SIR WILLIAM [Threatening]
Would you add conditions after the bargain is made? I must know your secret instantly.

MR BRONZELY
Then I will disclose it to you voluntarily; and rely on your honour to keep it.

SIR WILLIAM [Attentively]
Well, sir.

MR BRONZELY
Hark! I thought I heard somebody coming!

[Offers to go.

SIR WILLIAM
I insist upon the information.

[Laying hold of him.

MR BRONZELY
Well, then, sir—well—you shall—you shall.—Then, sir—in the small gallery, which separates the music-room from the rest of these apartments—in that little gallery, the lamp is just, unfortunately, gone out.—I was (as unfortunately) coming along, when the whisking of a woman's gown made me give a sudden start!—I found a person was in the gallery with me, and in the dark.

SIR WILLIAM
Well, sir!

MR BRONZELY
And so, confidently assuring myself, that it was Miss Dorrillon's waiting-maid, or Lady Mary's waiting-maid, I most unluckily clasped my arms around her, and took one kiss.

SIR WILLIAM
Only one?

MR BRONZELY
There might be half a dozen! I won't pretend to swear to one. We'll say half a dozen, before I knew who she was. My rapidity would not let her breathe at first, and she was fairly speechless.—But the moment she recovered her breath she cried, "Villain! whoever you are, you shall repent this:"—and I found it was the voice of a lady to whom I had just been introduced in the concert room, one Lady Priory! It seems, she was stealing to bed at the time we unhappily met.

SIR WILLIAM
But what has this to do with your coat?

MR BRONZELY
A great deal, sir—you will find, a great deal.—As I perceived she did not know me, I carefully held my tongue—but she, with her prudish notions, called "Help!" and "murder!" On which, I flew to the door, to get away before the lights could be brought—she flew after me; and, as I went out, exclaimed—"Don't hope to conceal yourself; I shall know you among the whole concert room; for I carry scissars hanging at my side, and I have cut a piece off your coat."—

[**SIR WILLIAM** looks hastily at his Coat—on which **MR BRONZELY** holds up the Part cut.

—And, sure enough, so she had!

SIR WILLIAM [In Anger]
And what, sir, am I to have the shame—

MR BRONZELY
Either you or I must.

SIR WILLIAM
And do you dare—

MR BRONZELY
Consider, my dear sir, how much less the fault is, if perpetrated by you than by me! This is the first offence of the kind which, I dare say, you have committed this many a year; and it will be overlooked in you. But I have been suspected of two or three things of the same sort within a very short time; and I should never be forgiven.

SIR WILLIAM
Nor ought you to be forgiven—it would be scandalous in me to connive—

MR BRONZELY
But would it not be more scandalous to reveal the secret of a person who confided in you?—who flew to you in distress, as his friend, the partner of his cares?

SIR WILLIAM
Your impertinence to me, but more your offence to a woman of virtue, deserves punishment. Yet I think the punishment of death, in the way that a man of my Lord Priory's temper might inflict it, much too honourable for your deserts; so I save your life for some less creditable end. I lend you my coat, to disgrace you by existence: and will go to my chamber, and put on another myself.

[Passes **MR BRONZELY**, in order to retire to his Chamber.

[Enter **LORD PRIORY**, who meets him. **SIR WILLIAM** starts.

MR BRONZELY [Going up to **LORD PRIORY**]
Ah, my lord! is the concert over? charming music! that solo was divine.

[**SIR WILLIAM** steals to a Chair, and sits down to hide his Coat.

LORD PRIORY [After looking inquisitively at Bronzely's Dress]
It is time the concert should be over—
[In great Anger]
—it had been better had it never begun; for there have been some very improper persons admitted.

MR BRONZELY [Affecting surprise]
Indeed!

LORD PRIORY [Trembling with Rage]
I am at a loss how to act.

[Draws a Chair with violence, and places himself down by **SIR WILLIAM**—**SIR WILLIAM** appears disconcerted and uneasy.

But if I could find the man to whom this piece of cloth belongs—

MR BRONZELY
What! that small piece of woollen cloth?

LORD PRIORY
Yes; then I should know how to act. In the mean time, Mr. Mandred, as I know you are a great admirer of my wife—

[**SIR WILLIAM** starts.

—and a grave prudent man of honour, I come to ask your advice, how I am the most likely to find out the villain who has dared to insult her; for a gross insult she has received from one of Mr. Norberry's visitors, wearing a coat of which this is a part.

MR BRONZELY
The villain, no doubt, stole out of the house immediately.

LORD PRIORY
I ordered the street door to be guarded that instant—and you, Mr. Bronzely, are now the last man whose habit I have examined.

MR BRONZELY
And you see I am perfectly whole.

[Turning round.

LORD PRIORY
I do see—I do see.

[**SIR WILLIAM** moves about on his Chair, and appears greatly embarrassed. **LORD PRIORY** starts up in a violent Passion— **SIR WILLIAM** starts up with him.

LORD PRIORY
I'll find him out if he be on earth—I'll find him out if—My passion carries me away—I have not coolness to detect him myself—I'll employ another—I'll send Oliver in search. Oliver!
[Calling]
Oliver! here, Oliver! Why don't you answer when you are called, you stupid, dull, idle, forgetful, blundering, obstinate, careless, self-sufficient—

[Exit, in a Fury.

SIR WILLIAM [Rising with great Dignity]
And now, Mr. Bronzely, how do you think you are to repay me, for having felt one transitory moment of shame? Understand, sir, that shame is one of the misfortunes to which I have never—

[Enter **LADY MARY RAFFLE**.

MR BRONZELY [Aside to **SIR WILLIAM**]
Sit down, sit down, sit down—hold your tongue, and sit down.

[**SIR WILLIAM** reluctantly retires to a Chair.

LADY MARY RAFFLE
Well, I do most cordially rejoice, when peevish, suspicious, and censorious people, meet with humiliation! I could die with laughing at the incident, which has put both my Lord and my Lady Priory into the greatest terror, grief, and rage.

SIR WILLIAM [Rising]
I am out of all patience. The malicious depravity of persons in a certain sphere of life is not to be borne.
[With Firmness and Solemnity]
Lady Mary—Mr. Bronzely—

MR BRONZELY [In a half Whisper to him]
Go away—don't expose yourself—steal out of the room—take my advice, and go to bed—hide yourself. So great is my respect for you, I would not have you detected for the world.

SIR WILLIAM
I am going to retire, sir. I would not throw my friend's house into confusion and broils; therefore I am as well pleased not to be detected as you can be.

[Goes to the Door, then turns.

But before I quit the room, I am irresistibly impelled to say—Mr. Bronzely! Lady Mary! while you continue to ridicule all that is virtuous, estimable, dignified, your vices most assuredly will plunge you into that very disgrace—

[Enter **OLIVER**, and places the Piece of Cloth against Sir William's Coat.

OLIVER
'Tis as exact a match as ever was—it fits to a thread. Ha! ha! ha!—Ha! ha! ha!

SIR WILLIAM
Rascal!

MR BRONZELY
Did not I entreat you to go to bed?

LADY MARY RAFFLE
Oh, this is the highest gratification I ever knew!
[Calling]
My lord! my lord!

MR BRONZELY
Hush, hush!—hold, for Heaven's sake.

OLIVER
But mercy and goodness defend us! who would have thought of this grave gentleman? Ha! ha! ha!—I can tell you what, sir; my lord will be in a terrible passion with you. This house won't hold you both; and I am sure I hate to make mischief.—Mum—I'll say nothing about it.

[Clapping **SIR WILLIAM** on the Shoulder.

And so make yourself easy.

MR BRONZELY [On the other side of **SIR WILLIAM**]
Yes, make yourself easy.

OLIVER
A good servant should sometimes be a peacemaker—for my part, I have faults of my own, and so, I dare say, has that gentleman—and so, I dare say, has that gentlewoman. But of all the birds in the wood, how came you to make up to my lady? ha! ha! ha! ha! ha!

MR BRONZELY
No jests—no jests. Mr. Mandred is my friend—my very good friend—and he is not so much to blame as you think for.—Good night, my dear sir.—Heaven bless you.—I thank you a thousand times.—Good night.

[Shaking Hands with **SIR WILLIAM**, and leading him towards the Door.

SIR WILLIAM [With steady Composure]
Good night.—Good night, Lady Mary.

[Exit.

OLIVER

Why, he never so much as once said he was obliged to me.

LADY MARY RAFFLE
I am sure, if you do not discover this to your master, I will.

OLIVER
Oh! as that old gentleman had not manners to say "Thank you for your kindness," I'll go tell my lord directly.

[Exit.

MR BRONZELY [Running after him.]
No, no, no—stop, Oliver. He is gone.

LADY MARY RAFFLE
What makes you thus anxious and concerned, Bronzely? Now, may I suffer death if, till I came into this room, I did not think you were the offender.

MR BRONZELY
I! I indeed!—No, if I could have been tempted to offend any woman in this house in a similar manner, it could have been none but you.

[Bowing.

LADY MARY RAFFLE
No, Bronzely, no; I have been too partial to you, to have any remaining claims—Hark! don't I hear Lord Priory's voice in a dreadful rage!

MR BRONZELY
Then Oliver has informed him. What shall I do to prevent mischief? Dear Lady Mary, as it is not proper for me to stay here any longer uninvited, do you run and try to pacify my Lord Priory. Tell him Mandred does not sleep here to-night; and in the morning you are sure he will make an apology.

LADY MARY RAFFLE
I will do as you desire—but I know Mr. Mandred so well, that I am sure he will not apologise.

[Exit.

MR BRONZELY
Then I will for him. Early in the morning, I'll wait on Lady Priory, and beg pardon in his name, without his knowing it. Yes, I have got poor Mandred into a difficulty, and it is my duty to get him out of it. And then, I shall not only serve him, but have one more interview with that heavenly woman.

[Exit.

ACT THE THIRD

SCENE I

An Apartment at Mr Norberry's

Enter **MR BRONZELY**, *followed by a* **SERVANT**.

MR BRONZELY [Looking at his Watch]
I am early, I know: but Lady Priory is the only person I wish to see. Is my lord with her?

SERVANT
No, sir, Lord Priory sat up very late, and is yet in bed.

MR BRONZELY
Acquaint Lady Priory, a person who comes on urgent business, begs to speak with her. If she asks my name, you know it.

[Exit **SERVANT**.

Pray Heaven she may bless me with her sight! Never was so enchanted by a woman in my life!—and never played such a trick in my life. I am half inflamed by love, and half by spite, once more to attempt her.

[Enter **LADY PRIORY**—he bows most respectfully—she courtesies.

MR BRONZELY
Lady Priory, I come—I come upon rather an awkward, yet a very serious business: it was my misfortune to be among that company yesterday evening, where an unworthy member of it, had the insolence to offer an affront to your resplendent virtue.

LADY PRIORY
I have some household accounts to arrange, and breakfast to make for my lord as soon as he leaves his chamber: therefore, if you please, sir, proceed to the business on which you came, without thinking it necessary to interrupt it, by any compliment to me.

MR BRONZELY
I will be concise, madam.—In a word, I wait upon you from Mr. Mandred, with the most humble apology for his late conduct, which he acknowledges to have been indecorous and unwarrantable: but he trusts, that, in consequence of the concession which I now make for him, the whole matter will, from this hour, be buried in oblivion.

LADY PRIORY
[Going to the Side of the Scene, and speaking.] If my lord be at leisure, tell him, here is a gentleman would be glad to speak with him—
[To **MR BRONZELY**]
I am sorry, sir, you should know so little of the rules of our family, as to suppose, that I could give an answer upon any subject on which my husband condescends to be engaged.

[Going.

MR BRONZELY
Lady Priory, stop. You can at least use your power to soften Lord Priory's resentment; and unless this apology is accepted, a challenge must follow, and possibly he may fall.

LADY PRIORY [Sighing]
Possibly.

MR BRONZELY
You are interested for your husband's life?

LADY PRIORY
Certainly. But I set equal value on his reputation.

[Going.

MR BRONZELY
Hear me one sentence more.—I cannot part from her.
[Aside]
Oh, I have something of such importance to communicate to you—and yet—I know not how!

LADY PRIORY
Then tell it to my husband.

MR BRONZELY
Hem—hem.
[Aside]
Oh, Lady Priory, if the insult of last night has given you offence, should you not wish to be informed of a plan laid for yet greater violence?

[She starts.

LADY PRIORY
Good Heaven!

MR BRONZELY
This is neither time nor place to disclose what I wish to say; nor do I know how to find an opportunity to speak with you alone, free from the possibility of intrusion; where I could reveal a secret to you, which is connected with your happiness—with your future peace.

LADY PRIORY
You alarm me beyond expression! I am going to my own house about twelve o'clock, for a couple of hours—follow me there.

MR BRONZELY
And I shall be admitted?

LADY PRIORY
Certainly—for you have excited my curiosity, and I am all impatience to hear what you have to communicate that so much concerns me!

MR BRONZELY
Promise, then, no person but yourself shall ever know of it.
[She hesitates]
Unless you promise this, I dare not trust you.

LADY PRIORY [After a second Hesitation]
I do promise—I promise faithfully.

MR BRONZELY
Your word is sacred, I rely?

LADY PRIORY
Most sacred.

MR BRONZELY
And you promise that no one but yourself shall know of the appointment we have now made at your house, nor of the secret which I will then disclose to you.

LADY PRIORY
I promise faithfully, that no one but myself shall ever know of either.

MR BRONZELY
Remember then to be there alone, precisely at—

LADY PRIORY
At one o'clock.

MR BRONZELY
And that your servants have orders to show me to you.

LADY PRIORY
I am too much interested to forget a single circumstance.

MR BRONZELY
Go now, then, to Lord Priory with Mandred's apology—and urge his acceptance of it, with all that persuasion by which you are formed to govern, while you appear to obey.

LADY PRIORY
I will present the apology as I received it from you; but do not imagine I dare give my opinion upon it, unless I am desired

MR BRONZELY
But if you are desired, you will then say—

LADY PRIORY
Exactly what I think.

[Exit.

MR BRONZELY
I'll do a meritorious act this very day. This poor woman lives in slavery with her husband. I'll give her an opportunity to run away from him. When we meet, I'll have a post chaise waiting a few doors from her house; boldly tell her that I love her; and—

[Enter **MISS DORRILLON**.

My dear Miss Dorrillon, I could not sleep all night, and am come thus early on purpose to complain of your treatment of me during the whole of yesterday evening. Not one look did you glance towards me—and there I sat in miserable solitude up in one corner, the whole time of the concert.

MISS DORILLON
I protest I did not see you!—and, stranger still!—never thought of you.

MR BRONZELY
You then like another better than you like me?

MISS DORILLON
I do.

MR BRONZELY
Do you tell him so?

MISS DORILLON
No.

MR BRONZELY
You tell him you like me the best.

MISS DORILLON
Yes.

MR BRONZELY
Then I will believe what you say to him, and not what you say to me.—And though you charge me with inconstancy, yet I swear to you, my beloved Maria,—
[Taking her Hand]
—that no woman, no woman but yourself—

[Enter **SIR WILLIAM**, and starts at seeing his **DAUGHTER** in such close Conversation with **MR BRONZELY**.

SIR WILLIAM [Aside]
How familiar!—my eyes could not be shocked with a sight half so wounding to my heart as this!

MR BRONZELY [Apart to **MISS DORRILLON**]

Hush! you have heard the story; but don't laugh at him now. He is in a devilish ill humour, and it will all fall on me. Go away.—It's a very good story, but laugh at him another time.

MISS DORRILLON

I don't believe a word of the story; yet, as a received opinion, it is an excellent weapon for an enemy, and I long to use it.

MR BRONZELY

Not now, not now—because I have some business with him, and 'twill put him out of temper.

[He hands her to the Door.—Exit **MISS DORRILLON**.

SIR WILLIAM [Looking steadfastly after her]

Poor girl! poor girl! I am not yet so enraged against her, but that I compassionate her for her choice!—Is this the man who is to be, for life, her companion, her protector!

MR BRONZELY

Well, Mr. Mandred, I believe, I have settled it.

SIR WILLIAM [Anxiously]

Settled what?

MR BRONZELY

At least I have done all in my power to serve you: perhaps you don't know that Mr. Oliver divulged the whole affair. But I have waited on my Lady Priory, and I do believe I have settled it with her, to manage it so with my lord, that every thing shall be hushed up. You may expect a few jests among your female acquaintance, and a few epigrams in the news-papers; but I verily believe every thing material is safe.— Is there any further satisfaction which you demand from me?

SIR WILLIAM

Not at present—a man is easily satisfied who possesses both courage and strength to do himself right, whenever he feels his wrongs oppressive. I have as yet found but little inconvenience from the liberties you have taken with me; and what, just at this time, far more engages my attention than revenge, is, an application to you for intelligence. Without further preface, do you pay your addresses to the young lady who lives in this house?

MR BRONZELY

Yes I do, sir—I do.

SIR WILLIAM

You know, I suppose, which of the two ladies I mean?

MR BRONZELY

Which ever you mean, sir, 'tis all the same; for I pay my addresses to them both.

SIR WILLIAM [Starting]

To them both?

MR BRONZELY
I always do.

SIR WILLIAM
And pray, which of them do you love?

MR BRONZELY
Both, sir—upon my word, both—I assure you, both.

SIR WILLIAM
But you don't intend to marry both?

MR BRONZELY
I don't intend to marry either: and, indeed, the woman whom I love best in the world, has a husband already. Do you suppose I could confine my affections to Lady Mary, or Miss Dorrillon, after Lady Priory appeared? do you suppose I did not know who it was I met last night in the dark? wherever I visit, Mr. Mandred, I always make love to every woman in the house: and I assure you, they expect it—I assure you, sir, they all expect it.

[**SIR WILLIAM** walks about in anger.

Have you any further commands for me?

SIR WILLIAM
Yes, one word more.—And you really have no regard for this girl who parted from you as I came in?

MR BRONZELY
Oh yes, pardon me—I admire, I adore, I love her to distraction: and if I had not been so long acquainted with Lady Mary, nor had seen my Lady Priory last night, I should certainly call Sir George Evelyn to an account, for being so perpetually with her.

SIR WILLIAM [Anxiously]
Do you think he loves her?

MR BRONZELY
Yes, I dare say as well as I do.

SIR WILLIAM
Do you think she likes him?

MR BRONZELY
I think she likes me.

SIR WILLIAM
But, according to your method of affection, she may like him too.

MR BRONZELY

She may, she may.—In short, there is no answering for what she likes—all whim and flightiness—acquainted with every body—coquetting with every body—and in debt with every body. Her mind distracted between the claims of lovers, and the claims of creditors,—the anger of Mr. Norberry, and the want of intelligence from her father.

SIR WILLIAM
She is in a hopeful way!

MR BRONZELY
Oh, it would be impossible to think of marrying her in her present state—for my part, I can't—and I question whether Sir George would.—But if her father come home, and give her the fortune that was once expected, why, then I may possibly marry her myself.

SIR WILLIAM [Firmly]
She will never have any fortune.—I came from India, lately, you know; and you may take my word, her father is not coming over, nor will he ever come.

MR BRONZELY
Are you sure of that?

SIR WILLIAM
Very sure.

MR BRONZELY
Then keep it a secret—don't tell her so—poor thing! it would break her heart. She is dotingly fond of her father.

SIR WILLIAM
Hah! how!—oh no, she can have no remembrance of him.

MR BRONZELY
Not of his person, perhaps: but he has constantly corresponded with her—sent her presents, and affectionate letters—and you know a woman's heart is easily impressed.

SIR WILLIAM
I never heard her mention her father.

MR BRONZELY
Not to you; but to us who are kind to her, she talks of him continually. She cried bitterly the other day when the last ship came home, and there was no account of him.

SIR WILLIAM
Did she? did she?
[Eagerly]
Ay, I suppose she is alarmed lest he should be dead, and all his riches lost.

MR BRONZELY

No, I believe her affection for him is totally unconnected with any interested views. I have watched her upon that head, and I believe she loves her father sincerely.

SIR WILLIAM [Wiping a Tear from his Eye]
I believe it does not matter whom she loves.

MR BRONZELY
By the by, she hates you.

SIR WILLIAM
I thought so.

MR BRONZELY
Yes, you may be satisfied of that. Yes, she even quarrelled with me the other day for speaking in your favour: you had put her in a passion, and she said, no one that loved her, ought to have any respect for you.

SIR WILLIAM
I am much obliged to her—very much obliged to her. Did she say nothing more?

MR BRONZELY
Only, that you were ill-natured, dogmatic, cruel, and insolent. Nothing more.—And say what she will against you, you know you can be even with her.

SIR WILLIAM
Yes, I can be even with her, and I will be even with her.

[Enter **LORD PRIORY**, and takes **MR BRONZELY** on one Side.

LORD PRIORY
I have accepted this man's apology:—I will not call him to a serious account; but he shall not escape every kind of resentment.—I am resolved to laugh at him; to turn the whole affair into mirth and good humour; at the same time to gall him to the heart. Good morning, Mr. Mandred: how do you do this morning, Mr. Mandred?—Let me go,
[Violently to **MR BRONZELY**]
I must joke with him.

MR BRONZELY
But neither your voice nor your looks agree with your words.

LORD PRIORY
Mr. Mandred, I did intend to be angry—but it would give too respectable an air to a base action—and so I am come to laugh at you.

[Enter **LADY MARY RAFFLE**.

And I am sure you, Lady Mary, will join even me, in laughing at this man of gallantry.

LADY MARY RAFFLE
Oh, I am absolutely afraid to come near the Tarquin.

SIR WILLIAM
You need not, Lady Mary; for there can be no Tarquin without a Lucretia.

LORD PRIORY
However, Mr. Mandred, it is proper I should tell you, I accept the apology you have made: but at the same time—

SIR WILLIAM [Hastily]
What do you mean my lord? I have made no apology.

MR BRONZELY
Yes, yes, you have—I called and made one for you.

SIR WILLIAM
Made an apology for me! You have just gone one step too far then; and I insist—

MR BRONZELY [Drawing **SIR WILLIAM** on one Side]
I will—I will—I will set every thing to rights. It would be base in me if I did not; and I will.

[Turns to **LORD PRIORY** and **LADY MARY RAFFLE**.

Yes, Mr. Mandred, I will retrieve your character at the expense of my own. I am more able to contend with the phrenzy of a jealous husband than you are.

[Enter **MISS DORRILLON** and **SIR GEORGE EVELYN**.

I am happy to see you—you are just come in time to hear me clear the grave, the respectable character of my friend Mr. Mandred, and to stigmatise my own.—My lord, vent all your anger and your satire upon me. It was I (pray believe me, I beg you will; don't doubt my word), it was I who committed the offence, of which my friend, the man I respect and reverence, stands accused—It was I who offended my Lady Priory, and then—

LORD PRIORY
It cannot be—I won't be imposed upon.

LADY MARY RAFFLE
But how generous and noble in him to take it upon himself!

MR BRONZELY [To **SIR WILLIAM**]
There! what can I do more? You see they won't believe me!—Tell me what I can do more? Can I do any thing more?—My feelings are wounded on your account, more than on my own, and compel me, though reluctantly, to quit the room.

[Exit.

SIR GEORGE EVELYN
I am at a loss which to admire most, the warmth of Mr. Bronzely's friendship, or the coldness of Mr. Mandred's gratitude.

LADY MARY RAFFLE
Oh! if it were not for that happy steadiness of feature, he could not preach rectitude of conduct as he does.

LORD PRIORY [Going up to **SIR WILLIAM**]
Eloquent admonisher of youth!

MISS DORILLON [Going to him]
Indeed, my rigid monitor, I cannot but express admiration, that, under those austere looks, and that sullen brow, there still should lurk—

SIR WILLIAM
Have a care—don't proceed—stop where you are—dare not you complete a sentence that is meant to mock me.—I have borne the impertinence of this whole company with patience—with contempt; but dare you to breathe an accent suspicious of my conduct, and I will instantly teach you how to respect me, and to shrink with horror from yourself.

[She stands motionless in Surprise.

LORD PRIORY
What a passion he is in! Compose yourself, Mr. Mandred.

MISS DORILLON
I protest, Mr. Mandred—

SIR WILLIAM
Silence!
[Raising his Voice]
Dare not to address yourself to me.

LADY MARY RAFFLE
Did you ever hear the like?—And I vow she looks awed by him!

LORD PRIORY
How strange, that a man cannot command his temper!

SIR GEORGE EVELYN
Mr. Mandred, permit me to say, I have ever wished to treat you with respect—nor would I be rash in laying that wish aside.—Yet, I must now take upon me to assure you, that if you think to offend every lady in this house with impunity, you are mistaken.

SIR WILLIAM
Sir George, if you mean to frighten me by your threats, I laugh at you—but if your warmth is really kindled, and by an attachment to that unworthy object,—

[Pointing to **MISS DORRILLON**]
I only pity you.

SIR GEORGE EVELYN
Insufferable!—
[Going up to him]
—Instantly make an atonement for what you have said, or expect the consequence!

SIR WILLIAM
And pray, Sir George, what atonement does your justice demand?

SIR GEORGE EVELYN
Retract your words—Acknowledge you were grossly deceived, when you said Miss Dorrillon was unworthy.

SIR WILLIAM
Retract my words!

SIR GEORGE EVELYN
Were they not unjust?—Is it a reproach, that, enveloped in the maze of fashionable life, she has yet preserved her virtue unsuspected? That, encumbered with the expenses consequent to her situation, she has proudly disdained, even from me, the honourable offer of pecuniary aid? That her fond hope still fixes on the return of an absent parent, whose blessing she impatiently expects? and that I, who have watched her whole conduct with an eye of scrutinizing jealousy, have yet only beheld that, which makes me aspire, as the summit of earthly happiness, to become her husband?

SIR WILLIAM
Young man, I admire your warmth.
[With great Fervour and Affection]
There is much compassion and benevolence, and charity, in sometimes mistaking the vicious for the virtuous;—and if in the heat of contention I have said a word reflecting on your character, I am ready to avow my error; and, before this company, to beg your pardon.

SIR GEORGE EVELYN
That is not enough, sir,—
[Taking **MISS DORRILLON** by the Hand, and leading her forward]
—you must ask this lady's pardon.

[**SIR WILLIAM** starts, and turns his Face away, strongly impressed.

SIR WILLIAM
Ask her pardon! Though I forgive some insults, I will not this.—Ask her pardon!—

MISS DORRILLON
Nay, nay, Sir George, you have no business with Mr. Mandred's quarrels and mine.—Reserve your heroic courage for some nobler purpose than a poor woman's reputation.

SIR GEORGE EVELYN

Point out a nobler, and I'll give up this.

LADY MARY RAFFLE
There is none so noble! And I wish, Sir George, you would undertake to vindicate mine.

LORD PRIORY
Come, Lady Mary, let us retire, and leave these two irritable men to themselves.

LADY MARY RAFFLE
Come, Maria, let us leave them alone. He'll teach Mr. Mandred to be civil for the future.

MISS DORILLON [In great Agitation]
Dear Madam, I would not leave them alone for the world!

LADY MARY RAFFLE
Then, my lord, you and I will; they have no offensive weapons; so we may venture to leave them.

LORD PRIORY
This comes of being too warm in conversation! This comes of being in a passion!

[Exeunt **LORD PRIORY** and **LADY MARY RAFFLE**.

SIR GEORGE EVELYN
While there is a female present, I have only to say—good morning, Mr. Mandred.

[Going.

MISS DORILLON [Catching hold of him]
For once I give up my pride to soften yours. Come, do not look thus determined!—I am sure Mr. Mandred did not mean to offend me; the words he made use of fell from his lips by accident.

SIR WILLIAM
They did not—I meant them—I mean them still—and I repeat them.

MISS DORILLON [To **SIR WILLIAM**]
Now, how can you be so provoking?—Nay, hold, Sir George,

[He offers to go.

you shall not go away with that frowning brow.

[She draws him gently towards **SIR WILLIAM**; then takes his Hand.

Nor you, with that sullen aspect.—Come, shake hands, for my sake.—Now, as I live, Sir George, Mr. Mandred's hand feels warmer and kinder than yours—he tries to draw it back, but he has not the heart.

[**SIR WILLIAM** snatches it away, as by compulsion.

Thou art a strange personage!—thou wilt not suffer me either to praise, or to dispraise thee.—Come, Sir George, make up this difference—for if you were to fight, and Mr. Mandred was to fall—

SIR WILLIAM
What then?

MISS DORILLON
Why, "I could better spare a better man."

SIR WILLIAM
How!

MISS DORILLON
I see you are both gloomy, both obstinate, and I have but one resource.—Sir George, if you aspire to my hand, dare not to lift yours against Mr. Mandred. He and I profess to be enemies: but if I may judge of his feelings by my own, we have but passing enmities.—I bear him no malice, nor he me, I dare be sworn. Therefore, sir, lift but your arm against him, or insult him with another word, and our intercourse is for ever at an end.

[Exit.

[**SIR GEORGE EVELYN** and **SIR WILLIAM** stand for some time silent.

SIR GEORGE EVELYN
Why is it in the power of one woman to make two men look ridiculously?

SIR WILLIAM
I am at a loss to know, sir, whether you and I part friends or enemies.—However, call on me in the way you best like, and you will find me ready to meet you, either as an enemy, or as a friend.

[Exeunt separately.

ACT THE FOURTH

SCENE I

A Hall at Lord Priory's

TWO SERVANTS discovered sitting—**ANOTHER** enters.

1ST SERVANT
Do you hear, Mr. Porter, you are to admit no person but Mr. Bronzely.

2ND SERVANT
Mr. Bronzely—very well—
[A loud rapping]

—and there I suppose he is.

1ST SERVANT [Looking through the Window]
Yes; that, I believe, is his carriage.—
[To **3RD SERVANT**]
—Let my lady know.

[Exit **3RD SERVANT**.

[Enter **MR BRONZELY**.

MR BRONZELY
You are sure Lady Priory is at home?

1ST SERVANT
Yes, sir, and gave orders to admit nobody but you.

MR BRONZELY
Has she been some time at home?

1ST SERVANT
Yes, sir; I dare say my lady came from Mr. Norberry's half an hour ago.

MR BRONZELY
Waiting for me half an hour—
[Aside]
—Show me to her instantly.

[Exit, following the **SERVANT** hastily.

SCENE II

An Apartment at Lord Priory's

Enter **MR BRONZELY** and **LADY PRIORY**, on opposite Sides.

MR BRONZELY
My dear Lady Priory, how kind you are, not to have forgotten your promise.

LADY PRIORY
How was it possible I should? I have been so anxious for the intelligence you have to communicate, that it was pain to wait till the time arrived.

MR BRONZELY
Thus invited, encouraged to speak, I will speak boldly—and I call Heaven to witness, that what I am going to say—

LADY PRIORY

No, stay a moment longer—don't tell me just yet—
[Listening towards the Side of the Scenes]
—for I wish him to hear the very beginning.

MR BRONZELY

Who, hear the very beginning?

[Enter **LORD PRIORY**.—**MR BRONZELY** starts.

LORD PRIORY

I have not kept you waiting, I hope. My lawyer stopped me on business, or I should have been here sooner.—My dear Mr. Bronzely—
[Going up to him]
—I thank you a thousand times for the interest you take in my concerns; and I come prepared with proper coolness and composure, to hear the secret with which you are going to intrust us.

MR BRONZELY

The secret!—yes, sir—the secret which I was going to disclose to my Lady Priory—Ha! ha! ha!—But my lord, I am afraid it is of too frivolous a nature for your attention.

LORD PRIORY

I account nothing frivolous which concerns my wife.

MR BRONZELY

Certainly, my lord, certainly not.

LORD PRIORY [Angrily]

Besides, she told me it was of the utmost importance. Did not you?

LADY PRIORY

He said so.

MR BRONZELY

And so it was—it was of importance then—just at the very time I was speaking to Lady Priory on the subject.

LADY PRIORY

You said so but this very moment.

LORD PRIORY

Come, come, tell it immediately, whatever it is. Come, let us hear it.—
[After waiting some time]
Why, sir, you look as if you were ashamed of what you are going to say! What can be the meaning of this?

MR BRONZELY

To be plain, my lord, my secret will disclose the folly of a person for whom I have a sincere regard.

LORD PRIORY

No matter—let every fool look like a fool, and every villain be known for what he is—Tell your story.

LADY PRIORY

How can you deprive me of the pleasure you promised? You said it would prevent every future care.

LORD PRIORY

Explain, sir.—I begin to feel myself not quite so composed as I expected. You never, perhaps, saw me in a passion—she has—and if you were once to see me really angry—

MR BRONZELY

Then, my lord, I am apt to be passionate too—and I boldly tell you, that what I had to reveal, though perfectly proper, was meant for Lady Priory alone to hear. I entreated your ladyship not to mention to my lord that I had any thing to communicate, and you gave me a solemn promise you would not.

LADY PRIORY

Upon my honour, during our whole conversation upon that subject, you never named my Lord Priory's name.

MR BRONZELY

I charged you to keep what I had to tell you, a profound secret.

LADY PRIORY

Yes; but I thought you understood I could have no secrets from my husband.

MR BRONZELY

You promised no one should know it but yourself.

LADY PRIORY

He is myself.

LORD PRIORY

How, Mr. Bronzely, did you suppose she and I were two? Perhaps you did, and that we wanted a third. Well, I quite forgive you for your silly mistake, and laugh at you, ha! ha! ha! as I did at Mr. Mandred.—
[Seriously]
—Did you suppose, sir, we lived like persons of fashion of the modern time? Did you imagine that a woman of her character could have a wish, a desire, even a thought, that was a secret from her husband?

MR BRONZELY

It is amazing to find so much fidelity the reward of tyranny!

LADY PRIORY

Sir—I speak with humility—I would not wish to give offence.—
[Timidly]

—But, to the best of my observation and understanding, your sex, in respect to us, are all tyrants. I was born to be the slave of some of you—I make the choice to obey my husband.

LORD PRIORY
Yes, Mr. Bronzely; and I believe it is more for her happiness to be my slave, than your friend—to live in fear of me, than in love with you. Lady Priory, leave the room.

[Exit **LADY PRIORY**.

Do you see—did you observe the glow of truth and candour which testifies that woman's faith? and do you not blush at having attempted it?—Call me a tyrant! Where are the signs? Oh, if every married man would follow my system in the management of his wife, every impertinent lover would look just as foolish as you!

MR BRONZELY
This is all boasting, my lord—you live in continual fear—for (without meaning any offence to Lady Priory's honour) you know you dare not trust her for one hour alone with any man under sixty.

LORD PRIORY
I dare trust her at any time with a coxcomb.

MR BRONZELY
That is declaring I am not one—for I am certain you dare not leave her alone with me.

LORD PRIORY [In a Passion]
Yes, with fifty such.

MR BRONZELY
But not with one—and you are right—it might be dangerous.

LORD PRIORY [Angrily]
No, it would not.

MR BRONZELY [Significantly]
Yes, it would.

LORD PRIORY
Have not you had a trial?

MR BRONZELY
But you were present. You constantly follow all her steps, watch all she says and does. But I believe you are right—wives are not to be trusted.

LORD PRIORY
Mine is.

MR BRONZELY

No, my dear Lord Priory, you must first become gentle, before you can positively confide in her affection—before you can trust her in a house, or in any place, alone.

LORD PRIORY [Hastily]
To prove you are mistaken, I'll instantly go back to my friend Norberry's, and leave you here to tell her the secret you boasted. Pay your addresses to her, if that be the secret—you have my free consent.

MR BRONZELY
My dear friend, I'll accept it.

LORD PRIORY
Ay, I see you have hopes of supplanting me, by calling me your friend.—But can you conceive now that she'll listen to you?

MR BRONZELY
You have given me leave to try, and can't recall it.

LORD PRIORY
But depend upon it, you will meet with some terrible humiliation.

MR BRONZELY
Either you or I shall.

LORD PRIORY
I shall laugh to hear you tumbled down stairs.

MR BRONZELY
You are not to remain on the watch here; you are to return to Mr. Norberry's.

LORD PRIORY
Was that the bargain?

MR BRONZELY
Don't you remember? You said so.

LORD PRIORY
Well, if that will give you any satisfaction—

MR BRONZELY
It will give me great satisfaction.

LORD PRIORY
Heaven forgive me, but your confidence makes me laugh. Ha! ha! ha!

MR BRONZELY
And yours makes me laugh. Ha! ha! ha!

[Enter **OLIVER**.

LORD PRIORY

Hah! What brings you here, Oliver? Lady Priory and I are only come home for a few hours.

OLIVER

I know it, my lord. I thought nevertheless I might be wanted.

MR BRONZELY

And so you are, good Mr. Oliver. Your lord desires you to conduct me to your lady in the next room, and acquaint her it is with his permission I am come to conclude the conversation which was just now interrupted.—Is not that right, my lord? Are not those words exactly corresponding with your kind promise?

LORD PRIORY

I believe they are.

OLIVER

—I am "to take Mr. Bronzely to my lady, and tell her you sent him."

[Exit **OLIVER**.

MR BRONZELY

Now this is perfect fashion: and while I step to Lady Priory, do you go and comfort my intended wife Lady Mary.

LORD PRIORY

I hate the fashion—and were I not sure you would now be received in a very unfashionable manner—

MR BRONZELY

No rough dealings, I hope?

LORD PRIORY

Oh, you begin to be afraid, do you?

MR BRONZELY

No—but I have met with an accident or two lately—and I am not so well acquainted with ancient usages as to know, in what manner a man of my pursuits would have been treated in former times.

LORD PRIORY

A man of your pursuits, Mr. Bronzely, is of a very late date; and to be shamed out of them by a wife like mine.

MR BRONZELY

Then we shall all three be old-fashioned.

[Exit, following **OLIVER**.

LORD PRIORY [Returning and looking anxiously after **MR BRONZELY**]

I am passionate—I am precipitate—I have no command over my temper.—However, if a man cannot govern himself, yet he will never make any very despicable figure, as long as he knows how to govern his wife.

[Exit, on the Opposite Side.

SCENE III

Sir William's Apartment at Mr Norberry's

Several Trunks and travelling Boxes.—**SIR WILLIAM** discovered, packing Writings into a Portfolio.

SIR WILLIAM
And here is the end of my voyage to England!—a voyage, which, for years, my mind had dwelt on with delight!—I pictured to myself a daughter grown to womanhood, beautiful! and so she is.— Accomplished! and so she is.—Virtuous! and so she is.—Am I of a discontented nature then, that I am not satisfied?—Am I too nice?—Perhaps I am.—Soothing thought!—I will for a moment cherish it, and dwell with some little gratitude upon her late anxiety for my safety.

[He walks about in a thoughtful musing manner.—A loud thrusting and rapping is heard at his Chamber Door.

[Enter **MISS DORRILLON** hastily and in affright.

MISS DORILLON
Oh, Mr. Mandred, I beg your pardon—I did not know this was your apartment. But suffer me to lock the door:
[She locks it]
—and conceal me for a moment, for Heaven's sake.

SIR WILLIAM
What's the matter? Why have you locked my door?

MISS DORILLON [Trembling]
I dare not tell you.

SIR WILLIAM
I insist upon knowing.

MISS DORILLON
Why then—I am pursued by a—I cannot name the horrid name—

NABSON [Without]
She went into this room.

MISS DORILLON [To **SIR WILLIAM**]

Go to the door, and say I did not.

SIR WILLIAM
How!

NABSON [Without]
Please to open the door.

MISS DORILLON
Threaten to beat him if he won't go away.

SIR WILLIAM
Give me the key, and let me see from whom you want to fly.—
[Commanding]
—Give me the key.

MISS DORILLON [Collecting firmness]
I will not.

SIR WILLIAM [Starting]
"Will not"—Will not, when I desire you!

MISS DORILLON
No—since you refuse me protection, I'll protect myself.

SIR WILLIAM
But you had better not have made use of that expression to me—you had better not. Recall it by giving me the key.

MISS DORILLON
If I do, will you let me conceal myself behind that bookcase, and say I am not here?

SIR WILLIAM
Utter a falsehood?

MISS DORILLON
I would for you.

[A hammering at the Door.

SIR WILLIAM
They are breaking open the door.—Give me the key, I command you.

MISS DORILLON
"Command me!" "command me!" However there it is.

[Gives it him.

And now, if you are a gentleman, give me up if you dare!

SIR WILLIAM
"If I am a gentleman!" Hem, hem—"If I am a gentleman!" Dares me too!

[Going slowly towards the Door.

MISS DORILLON
Yes. I have now thrown myself upon your protection: and if you deliver me to my enemies—

SIR WILLIAM
What enemies? What business have you with enemies?

MISS DORILLON
'Tis they have business with me.

SIR WILLIAM [To them without]
I am coming. The door shall be opened.

MISS DORILLON [Follows and lays hold of him]
Oh, for Heaven's sake, have pity on me—they are merciless creditors—I shall be dragged to a prison. Do not deliver me up—I am unfortunate—I am overwhelmed with misfortunes—have compassion on me!

[She falls on her Knees.

SIR WILLIAM [In great agitation]
Don't kneel to me!—I don't mean you to kneel to me!—- What makes you think of kneeling to me?—I must do my duty.

[He unlocks the Door.

[Enter **NABSON**—**MISS DORRILLON** steals behind a Bookcase.

SIR WILLIAM
What did you want, sir?

NABSON
A lady, that I have just this minute made my prisoner: but she ran from me, and locked herself in here.

SIR WILLIAM [With surprise]
Arrested a lady!

NABSON
Yes, sir; and if you mean to deny her being here, I must make bold to search the room.

SIR WILLIAM
Let me look at your credentials.—
[Takes the Writ]

—"Elizabeth Dorrillon for six hundred pounds." Pray, sir, is it customary to have female names on pieces of paper of this denomination?

NABSON
Oh yes, sir, very customary. There are as many ladies who will run into tradesmen's books, as there are gentlemen; and when one goes to take the ladies, they are a thousand times more slippery to catch than the men.

SIR WILLIAM
Abominable!—Well, sir, your present prisoner shall not slip through your hands, if I can prevent it. I scorn to defend a worthless woman, as much as I should glory in preserving a good one: and I give myself joy in being the instrument of your executing justice.—

[He goes and leads **MISS DORRILLON** from the place where she was concealed—she casts down her Head.

—What! do you droop? Do you tremble? You, who at the ball to-night would have danced lightly, though your poor creditor had been perishing with want! You, who never asked yourself if your extravagance might not send an industrious father of a family to prison, can you feel on the prospect of going thither yourself?

MISS DORILLON
For what cause am I the object of your perpetual persecution?

NABSON
Lor! Madam, the gentleman means to bail you after all: I can see it by his looks.

SIR WILLIAM
How, rascal, dare you suppose, or imagine, or hint, such a thing?

[Going up to him in Anger.

MISS DORILLON
That's right, beat him out of the house.

SIR WILLIAM
No, madam, he shall not go out of the house without taking you along with him. Punishment may effect in your disposition what indulgence has no hope of producing.—There is your prisoner [Handing her over to him.] and you may take my word, that she will not be released by me, or by any one: and it will be only adding to a debt she can never pay, to take her to any house previous to a prison.

[With the Emotion of Resentment, yet deep Sorrow.

NABSON
Is that true, my lady?

MISS DORILLON [After a Pause]
Very true. I have but one friend—but one relation in the world—and he is far away.

[Weeps.—**SIR WILLIAM** wipes his Eyes.

NABSON
More's the pity.

SIR WILLIAM
No, sir, no—no pity at all—for if fewer fine ladies had friends, we should have fewer examples of profligacy.

[She walks to the Door, then turns to **SIR WILLIAM**.

MISS DORILLON
I forgive you.

[Exit, followed by **NABSON**.

SIR WILLIAM [Looking after her]
And perhaps I could forgive you. But I must not. No, this is justice—this is doing my duty—this is strength of mind—this is fortitude—fortitude—fortitude.

[He walks proudly across the Room, then stops, takes out his Handkerchief, throws his Head into it, and is going off.]

[Enter **LADY MARY RAFFLE**—a **MAN** following at a distance.

LADY MARY RAFFLE
Mr. Mandred, Mr. Mandred!
[He turns]
Sir—Mr. Mandred—Sir—
[In a supplicating Tone]
I presume—I presume, sir—

SIR WILLIAM
What, madam? what?

LADY MARY RAFFLE
I came, sir, to request a favour of you.

SIR WILLIAM
So it should seem, by that novel deportment.

LADY MARY RAFFLE
If you would for once consider with lenity, the frailty incidental to a woman who lives in the gay world—

SIR WILLIAM
Well, madam!

LADY MARY RAFFLE
How much she is led away by the temptation of fine clothes, fine coaches, and fine things.

SIR WILLIAM
Come, to the business.

LADY MARY RAFFLE
You are rich, we all know, though you endeavour to disguise the truth.

SIR WILLIAM
I can't stay to hear you, if you don't proceed.

LADY MARY RAFFLE
My request is—save from the dreadful horrors of a gaol, a woman who has no friend near her—a woman who may have inadvertently offended you, but who never—

SIR WILLIAM
'Tis in vain for you to plead on her account—she knows my sentiments upon her conduct—she knows the opinion I have formed of her; and you cannot prevail on me to change it.

LADY MARY RAFFLE
Do you suppose I come to plead for Miss Dorrillon?

SIR WILLIAM
Certainly.

LADY MARY RAFFLE
No, I am pleading for myself. I am unfortunately involved in similar circumstances—I have a similar debt to the self-same tradesman, and we are both at present in the self-same predicament.

SIR WILLIAM
And upon what pretence did you suppose I would be indulgent to you, more than to her?

LADY MARY RAFFLE
Because you have always treated me with less severity; and because I overheard you just now say, you "should glory in delivering from difficulty a good woman."

SIR WILLIAM
And so I should.

LADY MARY RAFFLE
How unlike the world!

SIR WILLIAM
No—whatever the discontented may please to say, the world is affectionate, is generous, to the good; more especially to the good of the female sex; for it is only an exception to a general rule, when a good woman is in pecuniary distress.

[Exit **SIR WILLIAM**.

[Enter **LORD PRIORY**, humming a tune, but with a very serious face: he pulls out his Watch, with evident marks of anxiety—coughs—rubs his forehead—and gives various other marks of discontent and agitation.—**LADY MARY RAFFLE** observes him with attention, then sidles up to him.

LADY MARY RAFFLE
By the good humour you appear in, my lord, I venture to mention to you my distresses. I know the virtues of Lady Priory make my failings conspicuous; but then consider the different modes to which we have been habituated—she excluded from temptation—

LORD PRIORY
No—she shuns temptation. Has she not in this very house been compelled to make exertions? Has she not detected and exposed both Mr. Mandred and Mr. Bronzely?

LADY MARY RAFFLE
Bronzely! Bronzely! How!
[Aside]
Another rival?

LORD PRIORY
She has not done with him yet, I believe; for, to tell the truth, he is now with her at my house in Park Street. He taxed me with being jealous of my wife—to prove in what contempt I held the accusation, I left them together, and bid him make love to her.

LADY MARY RAFFLE
Is that possible?

LORD PRIORY
I can't say I would have done so rash an action, had I been married to some women—to you, for instance—but I have not a doubt of Lady Priory's safety: her mind, I know, is secure, and I have servants in the house to protect her from personal outrage. The only fear is, lest he should have received one; for 'tis now near two hours—
[Looking at his Watch]
—since I came away, and I have neither seen nor heard any thing of either of them!—But to your Ladyship's concerns.

LADY MARY RAFFLE
I am at this instant, my lord, in the power of an implacable creditor: and unless some friend will give bond for a certain sum, I must—I blush to name it—be taken to a prison.

LORD PRIORY
I am not at all surprised at the circumstance, madam: but it amazes me that you should apply to me for deliverance. You have a brother in town; why not send to him?

LADY MARY RAFFLE [Weeps]
He was my friend the very last time a distress of this kind befell me.

LORD PRIORY
Ask Mr. Norberry.

LADY MARY RAFFLE
He was my friend the time before.

LORD PRIORY
Mr. Bronzely, then.

LADY MARY RAFFLE
And Bronzely the time before that.

[Enter **OLIVER**.

LORD PRIORY
Ah, Oliver! I am glad to see you, my good fellow. Ah! what have you done with Mr. Bronzely?

OLIVER
Nay, my lord, that I can't tell. I can't tell what he has done with himself.

LORD PRIORY
How long has he been gone from my house?

OLIVER
He is not gone yet, as I know of; for none of the servants let him out.

LORD PRIORY
Not gone! and you can't tell where he is!

OLIVER
No, that we can't: we have looked in every room for him, and can't find him any where.

LORD PRIORY
Not find him!
[Recollecting himself]
Ho! ho! I thought how it would be—I thought he'd have some trick played him. Where's your lady?

OLIVER
That I can't tell neither. We have looked in every room, and can't find her.

LORD PRIORY
How!

OLIVER
'Tis as sure as I am alive. I and the butler, two footmen, and all the maids have been looking in parlours, chambers, and garrets, every crick and corner, and no where can we find either Mr. Bronzely or my lady: but, wherever they are, there's no doubt but they are together. Ha! ha!

LADY MARY RAFFLE
No doubt at all, Mr. Oliver.

LORD PRIORY
Together! together! and not in my house! You tell a falsehood. I'll go myself and find them.

OLIVER
You must look sharp, then.

LORD PRIORY
How came you to miss them?

OLIVER
I chanced to go into the next room, to see if there was a proper fire to get it well aired; I knew I had taken Mr. Bronzely to my lady in the inner room, and I had heard them both laughing not a quarter of an hour before; but now, all on a sudden, there was neither laughing nor talking, nor any noise at all—every thing was quiet.

LORD PRIORY [Anxiously]
Well!

OLIVER
And so I thought to myself, thought I, I'll sit down here; for my lady will be ringing soon: however, there was no ringing for a whole half hour; and so then I thought I would e'en rap at the door; but nobody called "Come in." So then I went in of my own accord; and there I found—

LORD PRIORY
What?

OLIVER
Nobody! not a soul to be seen!

LORD PRIORY [Affecting indifference]
Oh! she has been playing Bronzely some trick! She has been hiding him; and in some miserable place!

OLIVER
But why need she hide herself along with him?

[Enter **MR NORBERRY**.

MR NORBERRY
My dear friend, my dear Lord Priory, let me speak with you alone.—I come upon business that—

LORD PRIORY
You look pale! What is your business? Tell it me at once.

MR NORBERRY
It is of so delicate a nature—

LORD PRIORY

I know my wife is with Mr. Bronzely—I left them together. I know he is a depraved man; but I know she is an innocent woman.—Now, what have you to tell me?

MR NORBERRY

What I have just learnt from one of your servants. About a quarter of an hour after you left them, they stole softly out at the back of your house, ran to a post-chaise and four that was in waiting, and drove off together full speed.

LORD PRIORY

Gone! eloped! run away from me! left me! left the tenderest, kindest, most indulgent husband, that ever woman had!

LADY MARY RAFFLE

That we can all witness.

LORD PRIORY

I was too fond of her—my affection ruined her—women are ungrateful—I did not exert a husband's authority—I was not strict enough—I humoured and spoiled her!—Bless me! what a thick mist is come over my eyes!

LADY MARY RAFFLE

No, my lord, it is clearing away.

LORD PRIORY

Lead me to my room.

[He is led off by **MR NORBERRY**, exhausted with grief and anger.—**OLIVER** looks after **LORD PRIORY**, then takes out his Handkerchief, and follows him off, crying.

LADY MARY RAFFLE

Ha! ha! ha! Oh, how I enjoy this distress! Ha! ha! ha!

[The **OFFICER** who has attended her during the Scene, and kept at the further part of the Stage, now comes forward, and bows to her. She starts on seeing him—takes out her Handkerchief, and goes crying off at the opposite Side, he following.

ACT THE FIFTH

SCENE I

An Apartment at Mr Bronzely's

Enter **HOUSEKEEPER** and **FOOTMAN**.

HOUSEKEEPER
Dinner enough for twelve, and only two to sit down to it! Come home without one preparation—not a bed aired, or the furniture uncovered.

FOOTMAN
This is not the first time he has done so.

HOUSEKEEPER
No: for 'tis always thus when a woman's in the case. Well, I do say that my own sex are—

FOOTMAN
Hush! here they are. Run away.

[Exeunt.

[Enter **LADY PRIORY** and **MR BRONZELY**.

LADY PRIORY
Only twelve miles from London?

MR BRONZELY
No more, be assured.

LADY PRIORY
And you avow that I did not come hither by the commands of my husband, but was deceived into that belief by you.

MR BRONZELY
Still it was by his commands your servant introduced me to you; and, upon an errand, which I feared to deliver till I arrived at a house of my own.

LADY PRIORY
What is the errand?

MR BRONZELY
To tell you that—I love you.

LADY PRIORY
Do you assert, Lord Priory sent you to me for this?

MR BRONZELY
I assert, that, in triumph at your betraying to him our private appointment, he gave me leave to have a second trial. If, then, you have ever harboured one wish to revenge, and forsake a churlish ungrateful partner, never return to him more—but remain with me.

LADY PRIORY
And what shall I have gained by the exchange, when you become churlish, when you become ungrateful? My children's shame! the world's contempt! and yours!

[Smiling]
Come, come; you are but jesting, Mr. Bronzely! You would not affront my little share of common sense, by making the serious offer of so bad a bargain. Come, own the jest, and take me home immediately.

MR BRONZELY
Is it impossible for me to excite your tenderness?

LADY PRIORY
Utterly impossible.

MR BRONZELY
I will then rouse your terror.

LADY PRIORY
Even that I defy.

MR BRONZELY
Lady Priory, you are in a lonely house of mine, where I am sole master, and all the servants slaves to my will.

[**LADY PRIORY** calmly takes out her Knitting, draws a Chair, and sits down to knit.

MR BRONZELY [Aside]
This composure is worse than reproach—a woman who meant to yield would be outrageous.—
[Goes to speak to her, then turns away]
By Heaven she looks so respectable in that employment, I am afraid to insult her.
[After a struggle with himself]
Ah! do not you fear me?

LADY PRIORY
No—for your fears will protect me—I have no occasion for mine.

MR BRONZELY
What have I to fear?

LADY PRIORY
You fear to lounge no more at routs, at balls, at operas, and in Bond Street; no more to dance in circles, chat in side-boxes, or roar at taverns: for you have observed enough upon the events of life to know—that an atrocious offence, like violence to a woman, never escapes condign punishment.

MR BRONZELY
Oh! for once let your mind be feminine as your person—hear the vows—

[He seizes her Hand—she rises—he starts back.

LADY PRIORY
Ah! did not I tell you, you were afraid? 'Tis you who are afraid of me.
[He looks abashed]

Come, you are ashamed, too—I see you are, and I pardon you.—In requital, suffer me to return home immediately.

[He shakes his Head]

—How! are not you ashamed to detain me here?

MR BRONZELY

I was not this moment—But now you urge the subject, I think I am.

LADY PRIORY [Hastily]

Repent your folly, then, and take me home.

MR BRONZELY

Can you wish to go back to the man who has made this trial of your fidelity, and not resent his conduct?

LADY PRIORY

Most assuredly I wish to return. But if you deliver me safe, perfectly safe, from further insult, it will be impossible for me not to show resentment to Lord Priory.

MR BRONZELY

Why only in that case?

LADY PRIORY

Because, only in that case, you will make an impression on my heart—and I will resent his having exposed me to such a temptation.

MR BRONZELY

Oh! I'll take you home directly—this moment—Any thing, any sacrifice to make an impression on your heart.

[Calling]

William!—

—I'll take you home directly.

[Calling]

Here, John, Thomas, William—But, upon my life, it will be a hard task—I cannot do it—I am afraid—I am afraid I cannot.—Besides, what are we to say when we go back?—No matter what, so you will but think kindly of me.

[Enter **SERVANT**.

Order the horses to be put to the chaise; I am going back to London immediately. Quick! quick! Bid the man not be a moment, for fear I should change my mind.

SERVANT

The chaise is ready now, sir; for the post boy was going back without unharnessing his horses.

MR BRONZELY

Then tell him he must perform his journey in half an hour—If he is a moment longer, my resolution will stop on the road.

[Exit **SERVANT**.

I feel my good designs stealing away already—now they are flying rapidly.
[Taking **LADY PRIORY'S** Hand]
—Please to look another way—I shall certainly recant if I see you.
[Going]
—And now, should I have the resolution to take you straight to your husband, you will have made a more contemptible figure of me by this last act, than by any one you have led me to.

[Exit, leading her off.

MR BRONZELY [Without]
Tell the post boy he need not wait—I have changed my mind—I shall not go to London to-night.

A Room in a Prison

Enter **MISS DORRILLON** and **MR NORBERRY**.

MR NORBERRY
You ought to have known it was vain to send for me. Have not I repeatedly declared, that, till I heard from your father, you should receive nothing more from me than a bare subsistence?—I promise to allow you thus much, even in this miserable place: but do not indulge a hope that I can release you from it.
[She weeps—he goes to the Door—then returns]
I forgot to mention, that Mr. Mandred goes on board to-morrow, for India; and, little as you may think of his sensibility, he seems concerned at the thought of quitting England in resentment, without just bidding you a parting farewell. He came with me hither—shall I send him up?

MISS DORILLON
Oh, no! for Heaven's sake! Deliver me from his asperity, as you would save me from distraction.

MR NORBERRY
Nay, 'tis for the last time—you had better see him. You may be sorry, perhaps, you did not, when he is gone.

MISS DORILLON
No, no: I sha'n't be sorry.—Go, and excuse me—Go, and prevent his coming. I cannot see him.—

[Exit **MR NORBERRY**.

—This would be aggravation of punishment, to shut me in a prison, and yet not shelter me from the insults of the world!

[Enter **SIR WILLIAM**.—She starts.

SIR WILLIAM

I know you have desired not to be troubled with my visit; and I come with all humility—I do not come, be assured, to reproach you.

MISS DORILLON

Unexpected mercy!

SIR WILLIAM

No; though I have watched your course with anger, yet I do not behold its end with triumph.

MISS DORILLON

It is not to your honour, that you think necessary to give this statement of your mind.

SIR WILLIAM

May be—but I never boasted of perfection, though I can boast of grief that I am so far beneath it. I can boast too, that, though I frequently give offence to others, I could never part with any one for ever (as I now shall with you), without endeavouring to make some atonement.

MISS DORILLON

You acknowledge, then, your cruelty to me?

SIR WILLIAM

I acknowledge I have taken upon me to advise, beyond the liberty allowed, by custom, to one who has no apparent interest or authority.—But, not to repeat what is passed; I come with the approbation of your friend Mr. Norberry, to make a proposal to you for the future.

[He draws Chairs, and they sit.

MISS DORILLON [Eagerly]

What proposal?—What is it?

SIR WILLIAM

Mr. Norberry will not give either his money or his word to release you.—But as I am rich—have lost my only child—and wish to do some good with my fortune, I will instantly lay down the money of which you are in want, upon certain conditions.

MISS DORILLON

Do I hear right? Is it possible I can find a friend in you!—a friend to relieve me from the depth of misery! Oh, Mr. Mandred!

SIR WILLIAM

Before you return thanks, hear the conditions on which I make my offer.

MISS DORILLON

Any conditions—What you please!

SIR WILLIAM

You must promise, solemnly promise, never to return to your former follies and extravagancies.

[She looks down.

Do you hesitate? Do you refuse?—Won't you promise?

MISS DORILLON
I would, willingly—but for one reason.

SIR WILLIAM
And what is that?

MISS DORILLON
The fear, I should not keep my word.

SIR WILLIAM
You will, if your fear be real.

MISS DORILLON
It is real—it is even so great, that I have no hope.

SIR WILLIAM
You refuse my offer, then, and dismiss me?

[Rises.

MISS DORILLON [Rising also]
With much reluctance.—But I cannot,—indeed I cannot make a promise, unless I were to feel my heart wholly subdued; and my mind entirely convinced that I should never break it.—Sir, I am most sincerely obliged to you for the good which I am sure you designed me; but do not tempt me with the proposal again—do not place me in a situation, that might add to all my other afflictions, the remorse of having deceived you.

SIR WILLIAM [After a Pause]
Well, I will dispense with this condition—but there is another I must substitute in its stead.—Resolve to pass the remainder of your life, some few ensuing years at least, in the country.

[She starts.

Do you start at that?

MISS DORILLON
I do not love the country. I am always miserable while I am from London. Besides, there are no follies or extravagancies in the country.—Dear sir, this is giving me up the first condition, and then forcing me to keep it by the second.

SIR WILLIAM
There, madam,—

[Taking out his Pocket-book.

I scorn to hold out hopes, and then destroy them. There is a thousand pounds free of all constraint—

[She takes it.

—extricate yourself from this situation, and be your own mistress to return to it when you please.

[Going.

MISS DORILLON
Oh, my benefactor! bid me farewell at parting—do not leave me in anger.

SIR WILLIAM
How! will you dictate terms to me, while you reject all mine?

MISS DORILLON
Then only suffer me to express my gratitude—

SIR WILLIAM
I will not hear you.

[Going.

MISS DORILLON
Hear me then on another subject: a subject of much importance—indeed it is.

SIR WILLIAM
Well!

MISS DORILLON
You are going to India immediately—it is possible that there, or at some place where you will land on your way, you may meet with my father.

SIR WILLIAM
Well!

MISS DORILLON
You have heard that I have expected him home for some time past, and that I still live in hopes—

SIR WILLIAM [Anxiously]
Well!

MISS DORILLON
If you should see him, and should be in his company—don't mention me.

SIR WILLIAM

Not mention you!

MISS DORILLON
At least, not my indiscretions—Oh! I should die, if I thought he would ever know of them.

SIR WILLIAM
Do you think he would not discover them himself, should he ever see you?

MISS DORILLON
But he would not discover them all at once—I should be on my guard when he first came—My ill habits would steal on him progressively, and not be half so shocking, as if you were to vociferate them all in a breath.

SIR WILLIAM
To put you out of apprehension at once—your father is not coming home—nor will he ever return to his own country.

MISS DORILLON [Starting]
You seem to speak from certain knowledge—Oh, Heavens! is he not living?

SIR WILLIAM
Yes, living—but under severe affliction—fortune has changed, and all his hopes are blasted.

MISS DORILLON
Fortune changed!—in poverty!—my father in poverty?—
[Weeping]
—Oh, sir! excuse what may, perhaps, appear an ill compliment to your bounty; but to me, the greatest reverence I can pay to it.—You are going to that part of the world where he is; take this precious gift back, search out my father, and let him be the object of your beneficence.—

[Forces the Bank Note into his Hand.

—I shall be happy in this prison, indeed, I shall, so I can but give a momentary relief to my dear, dear father.—

[**SIR WILLIAM** takes out his Handkerchief.

—You weep!—This present, possibly may be but poor alleviation of his sufferings—perhaps he is in sickness; or perhaps a prisoner! Oh! if he is, release me instantly, and take me with you to the place of his confinement.

SIR WILLIAM
What! quit the joys of London?

MISS DORILLON [Kneeling]
On such an errand, I would quit them all without a sigh—and here I make a solemn promise to you—

SIR WILLIAM

Hold, you may wish to break it.

MISS DORILLON
Never—exact what vow you will on this occasion, I will make and keep it.

[Enter **MR NORBERRY**.—She rises.

—Oh, Mr. Norberry! he has been telling me such things of my father—

MR NORBERRY
Has he? Then kneel again—call him by that name—and implore him not to disown you for his child.

MISS DORILLON
Good Heaven!—I dare not—I dare not do as you require.

[She faints on **MR NORBERRY**.

SIR WILLIAM [Going to her]
My daughter!—my child!

MR NORBERRY
At those names she revives.—

[She raises her Head, but expresses great Agitation.

—Come, let us quit this wretched place—she will be better then. My carriage is at the door. You will follow us?

[Exit, leading off **MISS DORILLON**.

SIR WILLIAM
Follow you!—Yes—and I perceive that, in spite of philosophy, justice, or resolution, I would follow you all the world over.

[Exit.

SCENE III

Another Room in the Prison

LADY MARY RAFFLE discovered sitting in a dejected Posture.

LADY MARY RAFFLE
Provoking! not an answer to one of my pathetic letters!—not a creature to come and condole with me!—Oh that I could but regain my liberty before my disgrace is announced in the public prints!—I

could then boldly contradict every paragraph that asserted it—by—We have authority to say, no such event ever took place.

[Enter a **MAN** belonging to the Prison.

MAN
One Sir George Evelyn is here, madam; he will not name your name, because it sha'n't be made public; but he desires you will permit him to come and speak a few words to you, provided you are the young lady from Grosvenor Street, with whom he has the pleasure of being acquainted.

LADY MARY RAFFLE
Yes, yes, I am the young lady from Grosvenor Street—my compliments to Sir George, I am that lady—intimately acquainted with him; and intreat he will walk up.

[Exit the **MAN**.

This is a most fortunate incident in my tragedy! Sir George no doubt takes me for Miss Dorrillon; yet I am sure he is too much the man of gallantry and good breeding to leave me in this place, although he visits me by mistake.

[Enter **SIR GEORGE EVELYN**, speaking as he enters.

SIR GEORGE EVELYN
Madam, you are free—the doors of the prison are open—my word is passed for the—

[He stops,—looks around—expresses Surprise and Confusion.

LADY MARY RAFFLE [Courtesying very low]
Sir George, I am under the most infinite obligation!—Words are too poor to convey the sense I have of this act of friendship—but I trust my gratitude will for ever—

SIR GEORGE EVELYN [Confused]
Madam—really—I ought to apologize for the liberty I have taken.

LADY MARY RAFFLE
No liberty at all, Sir George—at least no apology is necessary—I insist on hearing no excuses. A virtuous action requires no preface, no prologue, no ceremony—and surely, if one action be more noble and generous than another, it must be that one, where an act of benevolence is conferred, and the object, an object of total indifference to the liberal benefactor.—Generous man, good evening.—Call me a coach.

[Going.

SIR GEORGE EVELYN
Stay, madam—I beg leave to say—

LADY MARY RAFFLE
Not a word—I won't hear a word—my thanks shall drown whatever you have to say.

[Enter the former **MAN**.

SIR GEORGE EVELYN
Pray, sir, did not you tell me, you had a very young lady under your care?

MAN
Yes, sir, so I had—but she, it seems, has just been released, and is gone away with the gentleman who paid the debt.

LADY MARY RAFFLE
Do you mean Miss Dorrillon?

MAN
I mean the other lady from Grosvenor Street.

SIR GEORGE EVELYN
Who can have released her?

LADY MARY RAFFLE
Some friend of mine, I dare say, by mistake.—Well, if it be so, she is extremely welcome to the good fortune which was designed for me. For my part, I could not submit to an obligation from every one— scarcely from any one—and from no one with so little regret as I submit to it from Sir George Evelyn.

[Exit, courtesying to **SIR GEORGE EVELYN**.

SIR GEORGE EVELYN
Distraction! the first disappointment is nothing to this last! to the reflection, that Miss Dorrillon has been set at liberty by any man on earth except myself.

[Exit.

SCENE IV

An Apartment at Mr Norberry's

Enter **LORD PRIVY**.

LORD PRIORY
What a situation is mine! I cannot bear solitude, and am ashamed to see company! I cannot bear to think on the ungrateful woman, and yet I can think on nothing else! It was her conduct which I imagined had alone charmed me; but I perceive her power over my heart, though that conduct be changed!

[Enter **MR NORBERRY**, **SIR WILLIAM** and **MISS DORRILLON**.

MR NORBERRY

My dear Lord Priory, exert your spirits to receive and congratulate a friend of mine. Sir William Dorrillon,—

[Presenting him]

—father to this young woman, whose failings he has endeavoured to correct under the borrowed name of Mandred.

SIR WILLIAM
And with that fictitious name, I hope to disburden myself of the imputation of having ever offered an affront to my Lord Priory.

[He takes **LORD PRIORY** aside, and they talk together.

[Enter **SIR GEORGE EVELYN**.

SIR GEORGE EVELYN
Is it possible what I have heard can be true? Is it Mr. Mandred who has restored Miss Dorrillon to the protection of Mr. Norberry?

SIR WILLIAM [Coming forward]
No, Sir George; I have now taken her under my own protection.

SIR GEORGE EVELYN
By what title, sir?

SIR WILLIAM
A very tender one—don't be alarmed—I am her father.

SIR GEORGE EVELYN
Sir William Dorrillon?

[They talk apart.

[Enter **LADY MARY RAFFLE**.

LADY MARY RAFFLE
Has there been any intelligence of my Lady Priory yet?

[Sees **MISS DORRILLON**.

My dear Dorrillon, a lover of yours has done the civilest thing by me!—As I live, here he is. How do you do, Sir George? I suppose you have all heard the news of Bronzely running away with—

MISS DORILLON
Hush!—Lord Priory is here.

LADY MARY RAFFLE
Oh, he knows it—and it is not improper to remind him of it—it will teach him humility.

LORD PRIORY
I am humble, Lady Mary; and own I have had a better opinion of your sex than I ought to have had.

LADY MARY RAFFLE
You mean, of your management of us; of your instructions, restrictions, and corrections.

[Enter **SERVANT**.

SERVANT
Lady Priory and Mr. Bronzely.

LADY MARY RAFFLE
What of them?

SERVANT
They are here.

LORD PRIORY
I said she'd preserve her fidelity! Did not I always say so? Have I wavered once? Did I not always tell you, that she was only making scoff of Bronzely? Did I not tell you all so?

[Enter **MR BRONZELY** and **LADY PRIORY**.

MR BRONZELY
Then, indeed, my lord, you said truly; for I return the arrantest blockhead—

LORD PRIORY
I always said you would; but how is it? Where have you been? What occasion for a post-chaise? Instantly explain, or I shall forfeit that dignity of a husband, to which, in these degenerate times, I have almost an exclusive right.

MR BRONZELY
To reinstate you, my lord, in those honours, I accompany Lady Priory; and beg public pardon for the opinion I once publicly professed, of your want of influence over her affections.

LORD PRIORY
Do you hear? Do you hear? Lady Mary, do you hear?

MR BRONZELY
Taking advantage of your permission to call on her, by stratagem I induced her to quit your house, lest restraint might there act as my enemy. But your authority, your prerogative, your honour, attached to her under my roof. She has held those rights sacred, and compelled even me to revere them.

LORD PRIORY
Do you all hear? I was sure it would turn out so!

LADY MARY RAFFLE
This is the first time I ever knew a woman's honour vindicated by the good word of her gallant.

LORD PRIORY

I will take her own word—the tongue which, for eleven years, has never in the slightest instance deceived me, I will believe upon all occasions. My dear wife, boldly pronounce, before this company, that you return to me with the same affection and respect, and the self-same contempt for this man—
[To **MR BRONZELY**]
—you ever had.

[A short Pause.

LADY MARY RAFFLE

She makes no answer.

LORD PRIORY

Hush! hush! She is going to speak.—
[Another Pause]
—Why, why don't you speak?

LADY PRIORY

Because I am at a loss what to say.

LADY MARY RAFFLE

Hear, hear, hear—do you all hear?

LORD PRIORY

Can you be at a loss to declare you hate Mr. Bronzely?

LADY PRIORY

I do not hate him.

LADY MARY RAFFLE

I was sure it would turn out so.

LORD PRIORY

Can you be at a loss to say you love me?

[She appears embarrassed.

LADY MARY RAFFLE

She is at a loss.

LORD PRIORY

How? Don't you fear me?

LADY PRIORY

Yes.

LADY MARY RAFFLE

She speaks plainly to that question.

LORD PRIORY
You know I love truth—speak plainly to all their curiosity requires.

LADY PRIORY
Since you command it then, my lord—I confess that Mr. Bronzely's conduct towards me has caused a sentiment in my heart—

LORD PRIORY
How! What?

LADY MARY RAFFLE
You must believe her—"she has told you truth for eleven years."

LADY PRIORY
A sensation which—

LORD PRIORY
Stop—any truth but this I could have borne.—Reflect on what you are saying—Consider what you are doing—Are these your primitive manners?

LADY PRIORY
I should have continued those manners, had I known none but primitive men. But to preserve ancient austerity, while, by my husband's consent, I am assailed by modern gallantry, would be the task of a stoic, and not of his female slave.

LADY MARY RAFFLE
Do you hear? Do you all hear? My lord, do you hear?

LORD PRIORY
I do—I do—and though the sound distracts me, I cannot doubt her word.

LADY PRIORY
It gives me excessive joy to hear you say so: because you will not then doubt me when I add—that gratitude, for his restoring me so soon to you, is the only sentiment he has inspired.

LORD PRIORY
Then my management of a wife is right after all!

MR NORBERRY
Mr. Bronzely, as your present behaviour has in great measure atoned for your former actions, I will introduce to your acquaintance, my friend Sir William Dorrillon.

MR BRONZELY
Mandred Sir William Dorrillon!

SIR WILLIAM

And considering, sir, that upon one or two occasions I have been honoured with your confidence—you will not be surprised, if the first command I lay upon my daughter, is—to take refuge from your pursuits, in the protection of Sir George Evelyn.

SIR GEORGE EVELYN
And may I hope, Maria?—

MISS DORILLON
No—I will instantly put an end to all your hopes.

SIR GEORGE EVELYN
How!

SIR WILLIAM
By raising you to the summit of your wishes. Alarmed at my severity, she has owned her readiness to become the subject of a milder government.

SIR GEORGE EVELYN
She shall never repine at the election she has made.

LORD PRIORY
But, Sir George, if you are a prudent man, you will fix your eyes on my little domestic state, and guard against a rebellion.

LADY PRIORY
Not all the rigour of its laws has ever induced me to wish them abolished.

MR BRONZELY [To **LADY PRIORY**]
Dear lady, you have made me think with reverence on the matrimonial compact: and I demand of you, Lady Mary—if, in consequence of former overtures, I should establish a legal authority over you, and become your chief magistrate—would you submit to the same control to which Lady Priory submits?

LADY MARY RAFFLE
Any control, rather than have no chief magistrate at all.

SIR GEORGE EVELYN [To **MISS DORRILLON**]
And what do you say to this?

MISS DORILLON
Simply one sentence.—A maid of the present day, shall become a wife like those—of former times.

Mrs Inchbald – A Short Biography

Elizabeth Simpson was born on 15th October 1753 at Stanningfield, near Bury St Edmunds, Suffolk. She was the eighth of nine children to John Simpson, a farmer, and his wife, Mary, née Rushbrook. The family were Roman Catholics.

Her brother was educated at school, but Elizabeth, like her sisters, was educated at home. Elizabeth also suffered from a speech impediment, a stammer.

Elizabeth's father had died when she was only eight, leaving her mother to take care of a large family. These were difficult times.

Despite the fact that she suffered from a debilitating stammer she was determined, from a very young age, to become an actress. She had loved theatre from her very first childhood visit.

As a young woman Elizabeth was tall and slender. But this beauty brought with it the many attentions of men. It was double-edged.

Elizabeth had written to the manager of the Norwich Theatre to obtain acting work. He had replied that he would welcome a visit for her to audition. For her young naïve years this seemed like a golden opportunity. However, in 1770 her family forbade her attempt to take on an acting assignment there. They had no such qualms with her brother George, who entered the acting profession.

In April 1772, Elizabeth left, without permission, for London to pursue her chosen career. Although she was successful in obtaining parts her audiences found it difficult to admire her talents given her speech impediment. However, Elizabeth was diligent and hard-working on attempting to overcome this hurdle. She spent much time concentrating on pronunciation in order to eliminate the stammer. She was known to write out the parts she wanted to perform and practice the lines to point of such familiarity that her impediment was banished. Her acting, although at times stilted, especially in monologues, gained praise for her approach, and for her well-developed characters. For the audience she came across as a real person, not just an actor performing a piece. Elizabeth would keenly study the performances of others before she herself performed.

In these early months Elizabeth was young and alone, and reportedly also suffered from the attentions of sexual predators.

In June, merely two months after arriving she accepted an offer of marriage from Joseph Inchbald, a fellow Catholic and actor. They had met before on her previous trips to London, usually to see her brother, George, acting on stage. He had written her several letters proposing marriage which she had declined. But now it seemed the most expedient way to make progress in her career.

By all accounts it was still an odd choice. Joseph was a so-so actor, and at least twice her age as well as being the father of two illegitimate sons. The marriage was to produce no children and was not the happiest of unions.

On 4th September of that year, 1772, Elizabeth and Joseph appeared for the first time together on stage in 'King Lear'. The following month they toured Scotland with the West Digges's theatre company. This was to continue for the next four years.

In 1776 they decided on a change of career and a change of country. They moved to France. Joseph would now learn to paint, and Elizabeth would study French. It was a short-lived disaster. Within a month all their funds were gone and a return to England was necessitated.

They moved to Liverpool, Canterbury and Yorkshire and acted for both the Joseph Younger's company and Tate Wilkinson's company in search of permanency and a recovery from their ill-fortune.

Completely unexpectedly Joseph died in June 1779. Despite her loss Elizabeth continued to perform across the country from Dublin to London and places in between.

In 1780, she joined the Covent Garden Company and played Bellarion in 'Philaster'.

In all Elizabeth's acting career was only moderately successful and lasted some 17 years. However, she appeared in many classical roles as well as new plays such as Hannah Cowley's 'The Belle's Stratagem'. Around the theatre she was known for upholding high moral standards. She later described having to fend off sexual advances from, among others, stage manager James Dodd and theatre manager John Taylor.

It was now in the years after her husband's death that that Elizabeth decided on a new literary path. With no attachments, and acting taking up only some of her time, she decided to write plays.

Her first play to be performed was 'A Mogul Tale or, The Descent of the Balloon', in 1784, in which she also played the leading female role of Selina. The play was premiered at the Haymarket Theatre.

'Lovers' Vows', in 1798, was based on her translation of August von Kotzebues original work and garnered both praise and complements from Jane Austen and was featured as a focus of moral controversy in her novel Mansfield Park. Although Austen's book brought more fame to Elizabeth, 'Lovers' Vows' initially ran for only forty-two nights when originally performed in 1798.

One of the things that separated Elizabeth from other contemporary playwrights was her ability to translate plays from German and French into English and to use them as a foundation. These translations were popular with the public and her talents in bringing the characters to life was instrumental in achieving this.

Her success as a playwright enabled Elizabeth to support herself and not need a new husband to carry out this role. Between 1784 and 1805 she had 19 of her comedies, sentimental dramas, and farces (many of them translations from the French) performed at London theatres, although it is thought she actually wrote between 21 and 23 in total depending on which account you think is most accurate. She is usually credited as Mrs Inchbald.

As well she wrote two novels; 'A Simple Story' was published in 1791 and once referred to as "the most elegant English fiction of the eighteenth century". 'Nature and Art' was published in 1796. Both have been constantly reprinted.

Her four-volume autobiography was destroyed before her death upon the advice of her confessor, but she left a few of her diaries.

In her later years she found time to do a considerable amount of editorial and critical work. In 1805, she decided to try being a theatre critic. This literary excursion, after the praise for her acting and more so for her writing, seemed to be a low point in her achievements. The reception to her work amongst her peer critics was low, one commented upon her ignorance of Shakespeare.

Her career from actress, to playwright and novelist was achieved in difficult times for women to accomplish such things. Indeed, whilst the theatre and its boundaries were quite strict she managed, in her novels, to explore political radicalism. Her good looks together with her passionate and fiery nature attracted a string of admirers but she never re-married. Despite her love of independence, she still desired and sought social respectability.

Mrs Elizabeth Inchbald died on 1st August 1821 in Kensington, London.

She is buried in the churchyard of St Mary Abbots. On her gravestone is written, "Whose writings will be cherished while truth, simplicity, and feelings, command public admiration."

Mrs Inchbald – A Concise Bibliography

Plays

Mogul Tale; or, The Descent of the Balloon (1784)
Appearance is against Them (1785)
I'll Tell you What (1785)
The Widow's Vow (1786)
The Midnight Hour (1787)
Such Things Are (1787)
All on a Summer's Day (1787)
Animal Magnetism (c1788)
The Child of Nature (1788)
The Married Man (1789)
Next Door Neighbours (1791)
Everyone has his Fault (1793)
To Marry, or not to Marry (1793)
The Wedding Day (1794)
Wives as They Were and Maids as They Are (1797)
Lovers' Vows (1798)
The Wise Man of the East (1799)
The Massacre (1792 (not performed)
A Case of Conscience (published 1833)
The Ancient Law (not performed)
The Hue and Cry (unpublished)
Young Men and Old Women (Lovers No Conjurers) (adaptation of Le Méchant; unpublished)

Novels

A Simple Story (1791)
Nature and Art (1796)

.

www.ingramcontent.com/pod-product-compliance
Lightning Source LLC
Chambersburg PA
CBHW021939040426
42448CB00008B/1140